THE
PATRIOT WAR
ALONG THE
MICHIGAN–CANADA
BORDER

Raiders and Rebels

SHAUN J. MCLAUGHLIN

Charleston — London

THE
History
PRESS

Published by The History Press
Charleston, SC 29403
www.historypress.net

The cover image of the Battle of Pelee Island and the back cover image
of the Battle of Fighting Island are two in a series of Patriot War battle
re-creations commissioned by Parks Canada in 1977 and painted by C.H.
Forster. *Courtesy Fort Malden Museum.*

First published 2013

Manufactured in the United States

ISBN 978.1.62619.055.9

Library of Congress CIP data applied for.

Notice: The information in this book is true and complete to the best of
our knowledge. It is offered without guarantee on the part of the author or
The History Press. The author and The History Press disclaim all liability
in connection with the use of this book.

Contents

Preface   5
Acknowledgements   7

1. Setting the Scene   9
2. The Rebellion Begins: December 1837   12
3. American Leaders Join the Fight: December 1837   28
4. Western Patriots Launch First Invasion: January 1838   42
5. Fighting Island Occupied: February 1838   57
6. Pelee Island Overrun: March 1838   65
7. Sutherland and Theller Face the Courts: March and April 1838   73
8. Lodges and Secret Societies Form: May–September 1838   79
9. Theller and Dodge Escape: October 1838   92
10. Windsor Invaded: December 1838   97
11. Prisoners Tried and Executed: January 1839   118
12. Upper Canada Releases Selected Prisoners: 1839–40   125
13. Rebellion Fades: 1839–40   129
14. Transported to Van Diemen's Land: 1839–50   133

Conclusion   153
Appendix I. What Happened To…   157
Appendix II. Men Hanged and Transported   167
Bibliography   175
Index   181
About the Author   191

Preface

The undeclared war between the American border states and Upper Canada, which saw that British colony attacked at least thirteen times between December 1837 and December 1838, was a historical oddity. The so-called Patriot War was not a conflict between nations; it was a war of ideals fought by like-minded people against the greatest military power of the time.

Rebellions in Lower Canada (now Quebec) and Upper Canada (now Ontario) flared up in November and December, respectively, in 1837. The British army and colonial militia quickly extinguished the uprisings. The rebels failed to gain wide support and lacked the training and strength to prevail. The insurgency should have ended before Christmas 1837. It did not.

The defeated rebels fled to the United States, where Americans of all social classes embraced them as heroes. Due to a unique confluence of American history and economics, tens of thousands of people offered money, provisions, arms and, sometimes, their lives in the pursuit of a Canadian republic. Many Americans regarded the British—still much despised—as despots to be driven from the continent once and for all.

The American government, led by President Martin Van Buren, never endorsed nor aided the conflict. It was the American people who declared war on Britain. The officers and men in the volunteer armies saw themselves as freedom fighters engaged in a just and noble cause. While men with dubious personal agendas infiltrated the senior ranks, the majority of men who fought, died and hanged acted on altruistic ideals, however misguided their mission may have been.

The Patriot War raged through the Great Lakes watershed from Michigan to Vermont. This book principally focuses on Patriot War events that occurred adjacent to Lake Erie in Michigan and Ohio and along the Detroit and St. Clair Rivers.

The text includes brief coverage of eastern Patriot War campaigns to give context and to highlight individuals who played major roles on both fronts. A companion book published by The History Press, *Patriot War Along the New York-Canada Border*, describes the Patriot War around Lake Ontario and the St. Lawrence River in detail.

Acknowledgements

I am grateful to historian John Carter for his help in identifying key sources and for reviewing the manuscript for accuracy.

Thanks to John MacLeod at the Fort Malden National Historic Site in Amherstburg for giving me a tour when the museum was closed and for supplying several key digital images from the collection.

Thanks to James Arnott and the Archives and Research Collections Centre at Western University in London for providing access to the Elijah Woodman Family fonds and digital images.

And once again, I appreciate the efforts of my local library in Mississippi Mills, Ontario, for securing books through interlibrary loans.

Chapter 1

Setting the Scene

The fact that bands of Canadian colonists in Upper Canada (now Ontario) took up arms in the pursuit of responsible government is not surprising given the political realities of 1837. That a legion of Americans took up their cause with force and vigor is initially puzzling.

For the previous fifty years, the two New World neighbors had charted very different paths.

Between 1780 and 1837, the United States population rose six fold from 2,780,400 to over 16,000,000. The count of states doubled from thirteen to twenty-six. Settlement had pushed civilization from the coastal plains west past the Mississippi River. Leading citizens and politicians, including Andrew Jackson (president from 1829 to 1837), trumpeted the virtues of political and economic freedom (mostly for white males), responsible government and westward expansion. The political culture encouraged individual freedom.

Britain's Upper Canada colony came into official existence in 1791 with 10,000 nonnative residents. Most were loyalist refugees from the American Revolution. By 1837, the count of residents climbed nearly forty times that number to 397,490. The colony's principal towns lay in a thin band along the shores of the St. Lawrence River, Detroit River, Lake Ontario and Lake Erie. The colonial economy and its politics were tightly controlled by a network of prominent men and their families. The political culture stymied individual freedom.

A two-tiered government ran Upper Canada. It had a Legislative Assembly elected by voters and an all-powerful executive council made up of prominent citizens, appointed and headed by a lieutenant governor. The executive council could and did disregard advice and legislation from the elected assembly.

By 1837, the colonial executive council represented an oligarchy of wealthy men, judges and high-ranking military officers. Rife with nepotism and patronage, they ran the colony often for their members' profit. Opponents called them the Family Compact.

In Upper Canada, a reform-oriented political party arose to argue for democratic reform. The few times that reformers formed a majority in the Legislative Assembly, the executive council ignored them at its pleasure. Eventually, a minority of reformers counseled open rebellion as the only path to representative government. The mood in Upper Canada in 1837 matched the temper in America in 1775 when colonists fired the first shots of the Revolutionary War.

While Canadian politics fumed in 1837, the United States society suddenly seethed with its own discontent.

After fifty-six years of growth and prosperity, America hit a wall in 1837. Rampant land speculation combined with a sudden distrust of banks and of the new monetary innovation, paper money, led to the Panic of 1837. English banks called in loans made to United States banks. Those banks held little real money—their assets being notes based on landholdings—and failed. Fortunes disappeared. Unemployment spiked and a five-year recession began. The recession spread into Upper Canada, where bad harvests in 1836 had already depressed its economy.

Besides financial upheaval, the 1830s saw a steady series of new social experiments and clashes of ideals in America. Organizations formed to promote temperance, trade unions, education reform, penal reform, asylums, abolition and female suffrage—all of which threatened established ideas.

Following the Texas Revolution (1835–36), many Americans, especially young men, envisioned themselves as political crusaders, gallant fighters for democracy. (That the Texas Revolution had much to do with Mexico's prohibition of slavery was not widely acknowledged then.)

In 1837, Americans along the border from Maine to Wisconsin still harbored enmity for the British government. Though fifty-six years had passed since fighting ceased in the American Revolution and twenty-three years since the War of 1812 ended, people in those states wanted the continent purged of any vestige of English despotism. And people blamed the English banks for causing the Panic of 1837.

Americans had no quarrel with Canadian colonists, who were kith and often kin. Immigration controls being rudimentary, citizens flowed between the nations at will. Cross-border business connections and marriages were commonplace. Many Upper Canada merchants and farmers had emigrated from the United States and brought their democratic ideals and republican views with them.

When you add the Texas Revolution's romanticism to a nation awash in new ideas and combine that with the destabilizing effects of a recession and a deep-seated grudge against the British, it is easier to understand why Americans took up the Canadian rebels' cause. Brothers in difficult times, the Canadian rebellion offered an opportunity for young men to be heroes and old men to kick out the monarchists.

Chapter 2

The Rebellion Begins: December 1837

Heated debate over democratic reforms in Canada escalated into armed rebellion first in Lower Canada (now Quebec) in November 1837. While Americans had little involvement, it represents the first shots fired in what would become the Patriot War.

In Upper Canada, a revolutionary spirit developed in rural areas of the colony around Toronto and London. What these two areas had in common were large populations of recent American immigrants drawn to cheaper land. They had experienced a representative government in the United States and resented the Family Compact's autocratic ways. Residents in rural areas felt left out of the decision-making process and believed the government ignored their legitimate needs.

Proponents of reform spoke out against the Upper Canada government at meetings across the colony. Rhetoric changed to rebellion on the outskirts of Toronto early in December 1837.

MACKENZIE ATTACKS TORONTO

In the colonial center surrounding Toronto, the disaffected looked to William Lyon Mackenzie for leadership. Driven by uncompromising political principles and a hatred of elitism, William Lyon spent his adult life trying to bring political reform to Upper Canada.

Mackenzie rose to prominence among reformers through his early newspaper, the *Colonial Advocate*. Unlike newspapers of today, it served largely to get his opinions into circulation.

In January 1829, he won a seat in the colonial assembly. Because of his continued Family Compact criticism, the loyalist-dominated assembly voted three times to expel him, and each time he returned in the next election. He became the first mayor of the new city of Toronto on March 27, 1834, but lost the 1835 election. In the pages of a second publication, the *Constitution*, Mackenzie continued to advocate for reform. But he grew increasingly impatient and uncompromising. He

Drawing of William Lyon Mackenzie, circa 1850.

toured the rural country around Toronto organizing groups of potential rebels. His views on democracy found favor among farmers of American origin. His influence reached down into the colony's western counties around the towns of Brantford, London and St. Thomas.

When Mackenzie, forty-two, learned that the rebellion in Lower Canada had started, he commanded his troops to gather north of Toronto for a march on that city. With all regular soldiers from the local barracks away fighting near Montreal, William Lyon felt his men could beat any militia assembled against them, especially in a surprise attack.

By December 4, between seven and eight hundred of Mackenzie's rebels, dubbed the Patriots, gathered on Toronto's outskirts by a tavern owned by John Montgomery. (While a reform sympathizer, Montgomery was no rebel—at least not then.) Though the rebels temporarily had the upper hand, they did not make a decisive early move.

At dusk on December 5, Mackenzie rode on a white pony at the head of his ragtag rebels. Near the city, a militia picket fired on the bigger rebel force. Rebel captain Samuel Lount lined his men up. The front ranks returned fire and dropped on their bellies instead of stepping aside or kneeling to reload, as was the custom. The ranks behind assumed those in front had fallen to

Sir Francis Bond Head.

musket balls and retreated in fear. Mackenzie and Lount hastened to the tavern and reassembled five hundred remaining men.

The next day, Mackenzie lost further advantage by robbing the mail courier in search of intelligence instead of pushing on to Toronto. That day, Colonel Allan Napier MacNab, thirty-nine, arrived from Hamilton with sixty troops. The lieutenant governor, Sir Francis Bond Head, placed Colonel MacNab in charge of the defense of Toronto.

On December 7, Colonel MacNab's defensive force marched out to attack Mackenzie's rebels at the tavern. The two armies met in the early afternoon. The loyalist militia, supported by cannon, overpowered the rebels within an hour and sent them running like scared rabbits. Colonel MacNab arrested Montgomery and burned his tavern.

An estimated two hundred rebel officers and men ran for the United States. Many never made it.

Running for his life, Mackenzie traveled from one safe house to the next around the western end of Lake Ontario. Sympathizers rowed him across the Niagara River to Grand Island, New York. Mackenzie arrived in Buffalo on December 10, 1837, knowing his rebellion had failed but not yet aware that the Patriot War had just begun.

DUNCOMBE GATHERS AN ARMY

In the western towns and counties of the colony, Dr. Charles Duncombe became a leading advocate for reform by 1837. Foiled in his attempts at peaceful change, Dr. Jekyll became Mr. Hyde.

Born in Stratford, Connecticut, in 1792, the eldest of the five children, Duncombe grew up in New York State. He married and fathered four children. He taught school for a time and then moved to New York City to study medicine. In 1819, the family immigrated to Upper Canada, where he practiced medicine in several towns. With his intellect and urban experience, his civic stature grew in the fertile pioneer communities. In 1824, Dr. Duncombe co-founded the Talbot Dispensatory at St. Thomas, the first medical school

A circa 1895 painting of Dr. Charles Duncombe by E.I. Hirst based on an existing miniature, circa 1860. Duncombe was described as handsome, somewhat small in stature and with a pleasing and dignified appearance. As a speaker, he had a winning manner in both private conversation and public debate. *Toronto Public Library*.

in Upper Canada. He became surgeon to the Second Battalion of the Middlesex militia in 1825. He joined the Masons in 1820, rising to grand master in 1836. He became a member of the influential medical board in 1832.

Duncombe's civic standing inevitably drew him to politics. The residents of Oxford County first elected him to the Upper Canada legislature in 1830. Ever the idealist, he led the legislature in social reform. In 1836, his report on lunatic asylums broke new ground, stating that people with mental problems should be treated in hospitals, not sent to jail. He issued a report calling for prison reform and a report that recommended changes to the education system to better fund schools and teacher education. While the Family Compact balked at his progressive ideas, later governments implemented most of his suggestions long after his departure.

Dr. Duncombe started out as a moderate, but that changed as he grew disenchanted with the Family Compact's control of the colony. In September 1836, he sailed to England with a group of reformers to take their complaints about the corrupt Upper Canada government to the seat of British colonial authority. The reformers believed Britain would fix their colonial governance problems if they just knew the facts. Senior ministers showed no interest. The snubs extended up to Charles Grant, 1st Baron Glenelg (aka Lord Glenelg), the Secretary of State for War and Colonies and, thus, the boss of all colonial governors. That bitter visit planted the seeds of rebellion in Dr. Duncombe's soul. He returned home to learn that his property had been devastated by fire and his son killed falling off a horse. Dr. Duncombe grieved and stewed in seclusion for nearly a year. When he emerged, the gentle social reformer had become a radical ready to accept any means to achieve reform.

DUNCOMBE LEADS REBELS

Dr. Duncombe came late to the ranks of armed rebels. Bands of men had organized for potential conflict throughout the autumn of 1837. Not until December 8 (a day after Mackenzie's raid on Toronto) did the doctor step in as titular head of the rebels in western Upper Canada. Fellow rebel commander Donald McLeod wrote in his memoirs that Dr. Duncombe took up arms upon hearing that the government had issued arrest warrants for him and others on a charge of treason. (Similar warrants appeared for anyone in Upper Canada thought to be an associate of Mackenzie.)

On December 10, Dr. Duncombe and other western rebels received erroneous news that Mackenzie had captured Toronto. The call went out to move. Over the next few days, companies of rebels from a dozen villages marched to join Dr. Duncombe near Brantford (southwest of Toronto). Between three hundred and five hundred strong, they began marching to join Mackenzie. Just like Mackenzie's mob in Toronto, they were ill-prepared for battle. They were not all armed with muskets, they had little in the way of provisions and their leaders were not military men. Had these deficiencies not been so obvious, Canadian historian John Charles Dent states the rebel army may have been far larger:

> [The rebels] *risked property, name and fame, life itself, in a cause which they deemed a righteous one. But they constituted but a small portion*

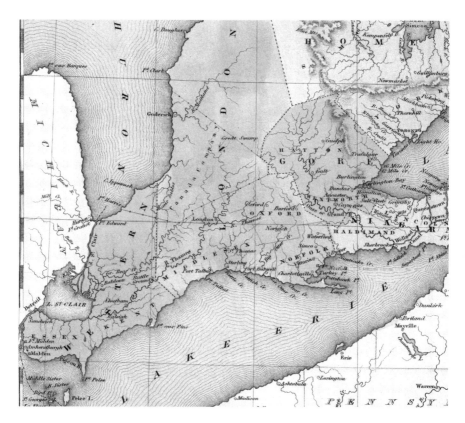

Map of Upper Canada in 1838 cropped to show only the western districts. Oxford County, in the center, was the scene of the Duncombe uprising in 1837. Essex County, on the lower left, took the brunt of Patriot attacks in 1838. Original by Thomas Bradford. *David Rumsey Map Collection.*

> *of the inhabitants, and their struggle was hopeless from the beginning. Hundreds—nay thousands—of farmers would have joined their ranks had there been a competent head to organize them and lead them to victory; but few were disposed to play for so heavy a stake with all the probabilities against them.*

On December 13, Dr. Duncombe received the truth about Mackenzie's defeat. He also learned that Colonel MacNab, with a loyalist army of at least three hundred plus one hundred Natives from the Six Nations Reserve, was closing in on his rebels. He urged his men to disperse. At first, several rebel leaders resisted and pulled the men southwest to the village of Norwich (south of present-day Woodstock, Ontario) for the night. By morning, most fighters had heeded the doctor's advice and disappeared.

PROCLAMATION.

REWARD.

By Command of His Excellency the Lieutenant Governor.

A REWARD is hereby offered, of

Five Hundred Pounds,

To any one who will apprehend and deliver up to Justice

CHARLES DUNCOMBE;

And a Reward of *Two Hundred and Fifty Pounds* to any one who will apprehend and deliver up to Justice, ELIAKIM MALCOLM; or FINLAY MALCOLM; or ROBERT ALWAY; and a Reward of *One Hundred Pounds.* to any one who will apprehend and deliver up to Justice, —— ANDERSON, (said to be a Captain in the Rebel Forces); or JOSHUA DOAN.

All the above persons are known to have been traitorously in arms against their Sovereign; and to entitle the party apprehending either of them to the Reward, he must be delivered to the Civil Power, At Hamilton, Niagara, London, or Toronto.

GOD SAVE THE QUEEN.

16th December, 1837.

A copy of the reward proclamation issued following the Duncombe uprising. Of the six men listed, Dr. Charles Duncombe escaped and never returned to settle, Eliakim Malcolm escaped and returned after his pardon, Finlay Malcolm was convicted but released a year later, Robert Always was jailed and released without trial, [David] Anderson died in battle and Joshua Doan hanged.

Some fleeing rebels joined the militia in the hunt for themselves—thus hiding in plain sight. Others surrendered to Colonel MacNab. He arrested leaders but released many of the ranks on their own recognizance.

Dozens of rebels fled to the United States to escape arrest. There they joined the Patriot forces gathering in New York, Ohio and Michigan.

Dr. Duncombe, with a £500 reward offered for his capture, traveled through forests and swamps in chilly winter weather. Friends and supporters assisted him to evade capture. He crossed over to Detroit six weeks later dressed as an elderly woman.

His frontline war efforts ended, but his behind-the-lines organizing continued.

Colony Rounds Up Rebels and Reformers

Mackenzie and Dr. Duncombe left behind a colony in upheaval. The rebellion gave the conservative "Tory" elite an excuse to crush its political opponents. Loyalist mobs terrorized the colony, tacitly encouraged by the Family Compact. That brutality and injustice forced many good and loyal citizens to flee to America, many into the ranks of the Patriot army.

In western Upper Canada, Colonel MacNab and other colonial leaders made no distinction between reform advocates and rebels. Innocent men who had merely called for democratic reforms crowded prison cells in Hamilton and London with those who actually bore arms.

Sitting members of the Legislative Assembly received no immunity if they showed any hint of rebel sympathy. MacNab's men arrested Robert Alway, forty-seven, a member for Oxford County, and Elias Moore, sixty-one, a Quaker elected in neighboring Middlesex County, both for allegedly encouraging people to take up arms.

Arrested men languished for months in filthy cells on flimsy charges. Most were eventually freed without trial. For several, their unwarranted incarceration served only to radicalize them and encouraged their later participation in the armed struggle.

WILLIAM PUTNAM

In 1795, Seth Putnam, who fought against the British in the American Revolution, moved to London, Upper Canada, from Pennsylvania. Two years later, his wife, Eleanor, and first child, William (born in 1794), joined him.

Like many colonists, the Putnams had all the earmarks of loyal citizens. William and his brother Joshua fought at the battles of Lundy's Lane and Queenston Heights, two pivotal Canadian victories in the War of 1812. William became a civic leader. For many years, he served as a captain in the London militia. He built mills and a distillery and operated a tavern. He bought property, farmed, held municipal office and became grand master of a Masonic lodge. But financial and political success did not make him complacent. He disliked the manner in which the Family Compact dealt with local matters. He became a follower of Mackenzie and was a participant at meetings in the London area to discuss reform.

On December 8, when word arrived of Mackenzie's assault on Toronto, Putnam attended a meeting of reformers in London to discuss what they should do in response. He urged everyone to go home peacefully and took his own advice.

According to a pamphlet written by his son Warner years later, his father, as a former militia captain, knew most of the officers who put down Dr. Duncombe's uprising. Those officers invited William for a few celebratory drinks at a hotel west of London. William gladly drank to the Queen's health but refused to toast the governor general, Sir Francis Bond Head. One captain berated Putnam and accused him of treason. In response, Putnam slapped the captain's face and ordered him to apologize or fight. Getting neither answer, Putnam went home, fetched his weapons and returned to the tavern. He repeated the challenge to anyone who doubted his loyalty. No one accepted.

On Christmas Day, a cavalry troop surrounded Putnam's house, arrested him without struggle and carted him off to the London jail. On February 4, 1838, someone set Putnam's farm buildings on fire. His family barely escaped alive.

A grand jury indicted Putnam on a charge of treason for his participation in an alleged conspiracy hatched at London. Despite that charge, the court released him on May 2, 1838.

A week later, a letter arrived from Mahlon Burwell, a personal friend and militia colonel. It stated that Putnam faced eminent re-arrest and counseled him to flee. Putnam boated down the Thames River to Lake St. Clair and arrived as a political refugee in Detroit. There he fell in with other rebels and refugees and began plotting his return.

MALCOLM FAMILY

The forces that shaped the rebellion often affected whole families. The best example is the Malcolm clan, which spawned thirteen rebels spread across generations. (There were three men in three successive generations with the given name Finlay involved in the uprising. They have been assigned Roman numerals to reduce confusion.)

Finlay Malcolm I (1750–1829) hailed from Aberdeenshire, Scotland. Later, as a sea captain and ship owner, he carried cargo between Scotland and America. He settled in Maine but moved to New Brunswick after the American Revolution. He arrived in Upper Canada in 1802. He had nine sons: Finlay II, Eliakim, John, James, Daniel, Peter, Duncan, George and Hugh. The family cleared farms and built mills near the towns of Oakland and Scotland (southwest of present-day Brantford, Ontario).

As loyal British subjects, Finlay I and two sons—Finlay II and John—served in the militia during the War of 1812. An American force attacked their area in 1814, defeated the local militia and burned John's mill. (The event is known as the Battle of Malcolm's Mill.)

The Malcolm clan prospered and multiplied. You could not travel the area without passing a farm, gristmill or tavern owned by one of the family. The men became leading citizens. Residents elected Finlay II to a term in the Legislative Assembly. Eliakim became a deputy surveyor in July 1821 and surveyed the village of Scotland.

As political tensions increased in 1837, the family tended toward political reform and became followers of Dr. Duncombe. John, Eliakim, Finlay II, his son Isaac and Finlay III (son of Daniel) spoke at protest meetings in local townships in 1837. James and Peter recruited men into the rebel force. When the call to arms came in December, the Malcolms gathered an estimated two hundred volunteers to support Dr. Duncombe.

A photograph of Eliakim Malcolm taken after he became the first warden of Brant County.

On December 7, the same day Mackenzie attacked Toronto, Eliakim held a recruiting meeting in a tavern owned by Joseph Beemer in the village of Scotland. One of the men who joined Eliakim was the tavern owner's son, Jacob Beemer, twenty-seven.

After crushing the Duncombe uprising, Colonel MacNab's officers discovered a buried chest on Eliakim's property containing a list of rebel names. Between December 23, 1837, and January 3, 1838, soldiers arrested three of Eliakim's brothers—Finlay II, fifty-eight; Peter, forty-one; and John, sixty-one—and four nephews—Isaac, twenty-five; Shubael, twenty-three; Finlay III, thirty-eight; and Norman, seventeen (locked up for protesting his father John's arrest)—and incarcerated them in the Hamilton jail.

With a £250 reward for his capture, Eliakim, thirty-six, managed to escape to Michigan. James, thirty-seven, also fled to America.

James's sixteen-year-old son, James Jr., was detained for questioning in December 1837 and released. Another Malcolm minor, Peter's son Augustus, seventeen, also briefly saw the inside of the jail. Eddy, twenty, son of Hugh, was arrested and released in December 1837 for a possible role in the Duncombe uprising and was again arrested and released in July 1838 over suspicions that he had joined another rebel incursion at Short Hills. (For details on that raid, see *Patriot War Along the New York-Canada Border*.)

Of all the living sons of Finlay Malcolm I, only Duncan, thirty-nine, and George, thirty-one, stayed out of the rebellion. (Hugh died in a barn-raising accident in 1828.) Daniel, sixty, avoided arrest, though evidence showed he urged men to take up arms.

Finlay II, John, Isaac, Shubael and Norman were among men released without trial in Hamilton in March 1838.

Peter, forty-one, was indicted as a rebel leader, convicted of treason and sentenced to hang on April 20 with five other rebels. Lieutenant Governor George Arthur canceled those executions. He'd executed two of Mackenzie's officers on April 13, and he believed the necessary examples had been made. The court then commuted Peter's sentence to fourteen years in a penal colony, but in November 1838, the court released him on £500 bail.

Finlay III was tried for being a rebel organizer, sentenced to fourteen years in the Van Diemen's Land penal colony (renamed Tasmania on January 1, 1856) and sent to England to await a southbound ship. While incarcerated in Liverpool, he and other convicted Patriots peppered English officials, jurists and newspapers with a fierce letter-writing campaign in the early months of 1839. They argued strenuously that their imprisonment was unconstitutional. Finlay and eight others succeeded in getting acquittals and came home.

James returned under a pardon in 1841. The following year, Eliakim received his pardon and came home. Considering the family's deep involvement in the uprising, everyone survived unscathed.

Eliakim and many other rebellious Malcolms are buried in the cemetery in Scotland, Ontario, and the lettering on their markers is still legible. Finlay I and his son John are in the pioneer cemetery in nearby Oakland, though time has erased their names on the old headstones.

BEDFORD BROTHERS

Among Dr. Duncombe's rebel forces were Paul Bedford, thirty-three, and his brother Daniel, twenty-five. Born in a rural township east of Toronto, they later moved to Norwich in western Upper Canada. Paul was a farmer and Daniel an innkeeper. Both were married men with young families.

In early December 1837, as many as one hundred men from the Norwich area joined Dr. Duncombe's uprising, including the Bedford brothers—Paul as a captain, and Daniel as a sergeant. They arrived just before Dr. Duncombe disbanded the army. Militia forces found a list of rebel names at one of Dr. Duncombe's properties. They arrested both brothers in mid-December during the clampdown on rebels and sympathizers.

Drawing from an 1839 issue of the *London Sun* showing rebel prisoners who appealed their transport sentences. *From left*: Paul Bedford, Linus Miller, William Reynolds (aka David Deal), Finlay Malcolm III, John G. Parker, Randal Wixon, Leonard Watson, Ira Anderson, William Alves, James Brown, Robert Walker and John Grant. Of these, all received pardons except Miller and Grant.

Magistrates released Daniel on bail on January 9, 1838. He shortly departed for America and joined other Canadian refugees in the Patriot army. He intended to keep fighting.

Because Paul was an officer, the court convicted him to transport for life in the Van Diemen's Land penal colony and sent him to England to await a ship. Like Finlay Malcolm III and seven others, Paul was acquitted by the English courts in 1839 and came home.

Doan Brothers

Joshua Gwillen Doan was born in western Upper Canada shortly after the family moved from Pennsylvania in 1811. His father, Jonathan, founded the Quaker community of Sparta (southeast of present-day St. Thomas, Ontario) where Joshua grew up. Like his father, Joshua became a farmer. In 1832, he and his brother Joel started a tannery. In 1836, Joshua wed Fanny Milard. The couple had one son.

The reform movement as espoused by Mackenzie and Dr. Duncombe stirred the brothers' souls. They abandoned their non-violent Quaker teachings and took up arms. Joshua became an officer in the rebel army and raised a company named the Spartan Rangers. Under David Anderson, an Irish-born innkeeper and local rebel leader, they marched to join Dr. Duncombe. After Colonel MacNab dispersed the rebels, Joshua, twenty-six, and Joel, twenty-four, fled to the United States. The British posted a £100 reward for Joshua's capture. Not intimidated, Joshua joined the Patriot army in Michigan. Joel kept a low profile.

According to the memoirs of Patriot general Dr. Edward Alexander Theller, Joshua Doan served in the Patriot force that attempted to attack Fort Malden near Amherstburg, Upper Canada, in early January 1838. That was not his only military foray into Upper Canada.

Elijah Woodman

Elijah Woodman was born in Buxton, Maine, on September 22, 1797. He became a farmer and lumberman. He came to Upper Canada in 1831 with his wife, Apphia, and six children in search of opportunity. A seventh child was born in Canada.

Woodman established a lumber mill on Otter Creek near the present-day town of Tillsonburg. With old-growth timber then massively abundant, and with Canadian and American towns rapidly expanding, he prospered for a few years. He was described as five feet, four and a half inches in height with a dark complexion, black hair and beard, a long head, a high forehead and hazel eyes. In 1836, he moved to London, Ontario, then a small town of one thousand. The Panic of 1837 hit the economy of Upper Canada almost as hard as it did the United States. Stuck with stacks of lumber he could not sell, he went bankrupt.

When the Upper Canada rebellion began in late 1837, Woodman stayed out of the local uprising led by Dr. Charles Duncombe. But Woodman could not ignore the backlash. The colonial government soon arrested

This drawing of Elijah Woodman from 1845 includes a typewritten description added later. *Courtesy of the Elijah Woodman Family Fonds, Western Archives, Western University.*

almost anyone who favored government reform. That heavy-handed response offended Woodman's American-inspired democratic views.

Several men arrested in London were, like Woodman, members of the Masonic lodge. As a humanitarian and Mason, Woodman felt duty bound to provide aid. He helped prisoners gather defense witnesses, he bore messages to and from their families and he witnessed trials in March 1838. Such activities attracted the suspicions of local Tory authorities. This they added to Woodman's list of other sins: his American roots, his failure to seek citizenship after seven years in the colony and his membership in the Universalist church. Members of colonial Canada's established churches despised upstart, American-based religious orders.

Viewed as a security threat, the authorities accused Woodman of passing knives and files to prisoners. He became a prisoner himself in June 1838.

Never tried, the courts released him in August only to re-arrest him days later. In late August, the jail doors opened again, and he fled to America.

In his later writing, Woodman stated, "These rascally proceedings made me a rebel."

Lewis Adelbert Norton

Among the rebel privates was a street-smart, seventeen-year-old adventurer named Lewis Adelbert Norton. He left home shortly after his eleventh birthday, as he explained later in his memoirs:

> *As my parents were poor and had a large family, I was determined to look out for myself. Early on the second day of May, 1829, I tied my worldly possessions in a pocket handkerchief, strung it over my shoulder, and, like a young quail with a shell on its back, I left the nest with twenty-five cents in my pocket.*

Norton worked on Lake Erie ships and on farms on both sides of the border. Along the way, he learned to read and write. He enlisted in the rebel company of Joshua Doan in the village of Sparta. On December 12, he answered the call to arms and began an eastward march under Doan and David Anderson.

Image of Lewis Adelbert Norton taken from his 1887 autobiography.

The next morning, Norton claims a band of militia—"twenty-five or thirty fellows"—ambushed their column. He says he took a musket ball in his back and scrambled to cover in nearby trees while his comrades repelled the attackers. (This is likely Norton's imagination or faulty memory at work. While a militia troop did attempt to ambush Anderson's column, they failed to cross paths.)

That evening, Norton and the other Spartan

Rangers joined Dr. Duncombe's main force in retreat at Norwich. Overnight, the army vanished.

> *The next morning, when I awoke, our command had disappeared, and I found myself comparatively alone. I saw some notices posted which were to the effect that a superior force was upon us, too formidable for us to attempt to cope with, and advising every man to look out for himself.*

Norton and another man spent two days in hiding before being arrested. Their captors took them south to join other rebel prisoners in the new jail in the village of Simcoe. Norton claims he helped two prisoners escape, and that act of gallantry cost him the early release that other teenage rebels received.

Authorities transferred Norton and other Simcoe prisoners to the crowded jail in London. For two weeks, he was interrogated daily by magistrates, who asked questions about specific rebels and their activities. He played the fool or refused to answer.

Norton is one of many chroniclers to describe the London jail's poor conditions and food. He stated that they had no blankets to fend off the cold Canadian winter for the first month and that the food was inadequate:

> *Each man was entitled to eight ounces of meat per day, and one pound of bread. But contractors were as rascally then as now, and the meat was saved up for outsiders, while enormous bones were weighed out to the prisoners. And as for bread, the stuff furnished us was a burlesque upon the name of bread.*

Prisoners left the jail—"either convicted and banished to the penal colonies, hung, or acquitted"—until just nine remained in Norton's block. In late summer, a magistrate released him on the condition that he leave Upper Canada and never return. Norton journeyed to Michigan, where he helped recruit men for the Patriot army, but he stayed out of further battles.

Chapter 3

American Leaders Join the Fight: December 1837

Rebels lucky enough to escape to America after the Mackenzie and Duncombe uprisings found prominent men not only enthusiastic in their welcome but also already organized to assist the cause of Canadian liberty. In Buffalo, New York, thousands rallied to Mackenzie. Dr. Duncombe and his rebel refugees encountered a similar welcome in Detroit, Michigan.

The reform movement in Upper Canada had not gone unnoticed in the Great Lakes states. A Canadian rebellion seemed inevitable to those watching the colony's reform agitations. Aiding the rebels appealed to many Americans, though motivations varied from altruistic to blatant greed and included spreading the blessings of democracy, expanding the borders of the United States, getting back at Britain and land speculation.

In Buffalo, a knot of prominent men had followed the rise of revolution in the Canadian colonies. Within days of Mackenzie's arrival there as a refugee, they paraded a very willing William Lyon before the public.

On December 12, 1837, Mackenzie explained to three thousand people in a packed Buffalo theater (the population of Buffalo was then twenty-five thousand) about the rebellion's causes. He compared the suffering of Canadians to the "same evils" that caused the thirteen colonies to break allegiance from England.

THOMAS JEFFERSON SUTHERLAND

The same evening, Thomas Jefferson Sutherland, thirty-six, addressed the throng after Mackenzie.

Sutherland had kicked around New York State for decades racking up minor accomplishments. He enlisted in the U.S. Marines in 1821 and was discharged with the rank of sergeant in 1830. He started the Troy *Statesman* weekly newspaper in June 1832. It served as a platform for his political and anti-Mason views. (Being against Masons was popular then.) The *Statesman* folded in 1834. He continued for several years as publisher or editor of short-lived newspapers in various towns. Documents also list him as being a lawyer as early as 1833.

The idealistic Sutherland closely followed the polemics of Mackenzie in 1837 and correctly surmised that Upper Canada lay on the verge of open rebellion. Two days before Mackenzie's botched assault on Toronto, Sutherland traveled there with a letter of support from sympathetic Americans (a trip he later denied happened).

Sutherland, as a writer and former sergeant, had both the power of the pen and sword at his disposal. A tall man weighing over two hundred pounds, he presented an imposing figure. He fancied himself a natural commander of men and fully expected to be a general in any force raised to win Canadian freedom. That night in Buffalo, he exclaimed to the audience that he intended to form an army of liberation. He requested men, money, ammunition and weapons. The response was immediate and generous.

One of the men who listened to Mackenzie and Sutherland speak at the Buffalo theater that evening was Samuel Wood, forty-three, a shipwright working on the Erie Canal. He later related the following in a legal deposition:

> *They both made long speeches there, representing that Canada was so oppressed, that it was impossible to live under the Government; that the Canadians were all ready for revolt, and that it was only necessary that a force from the United States should show itself, to cause a general rising of the people of Upper Canada.*

RENSSELAER VAN RENSSELAER

The next evening, December 13, Mackenzie and Sutherland met in Buffalo's elegant Eagle Tavern to plan a war. With them was Rensselaer Van Rensselaer, thirty-five. He came from one of the most influential families in upstate New York. Men with his surname ranked among the elites in politics and the military.

On December 11, 1838, while in Buffalo on business, Van Rensselaer met Sutherland. The latter immediately tried to recruit him into the Patriot cause. Sutherland offered to resign his position as Patriot army commander-in-chief to make way for Van Rensselaer. Sutherland believed the cause needed a person better known than he to impart "a proper tone to the enterprise." Van Rensselaer accepted at the request of Mackenzie, though he had no battle experience.

NAVY ISLAND OCCUPIED

The Patriot leaders agreed to occupy Navy Island and make it the seat of a provisional Canadian government in exile. The three-hundred-acre island in the Niagara River, not far from the mighty falls, belonged to Upper Canada.

On December 14, 1837, Mackenzie and newly appointed top general Van Rensselaer landed on Navy Island by way of Grand Island with twenty-four volunteers and two small cannons.

Samuel Wood claimed he joined the first brigade of men to occupy Navy Island. His account from a legal deposition follows:

> *Mackenzie and Sutherland had, to my knowledge, at that time, only twenty-seven followers, of whom I was the first to join them. I held no rank but was promised great advantages in my trade of shipwright when Canada should be conquered. We went from Tonawanda to Black Rock, on the night of the 11th, between eleven and twelve o'clock. On the morning of the 12th, we went to a store at Black Rock; here we found 400 stand of arms, muskets, bayonets, and accoutrements: they bore the Springfield mark. There is a large manufactory at Springfield, where arms are made for the United States Government. The arms were, I understood, brought there in the night; but I never learned where they came from, or by whom they were placed there. At the first formation of the patriots, there were no oaths administered, but many of the proceedings were kept secret from*

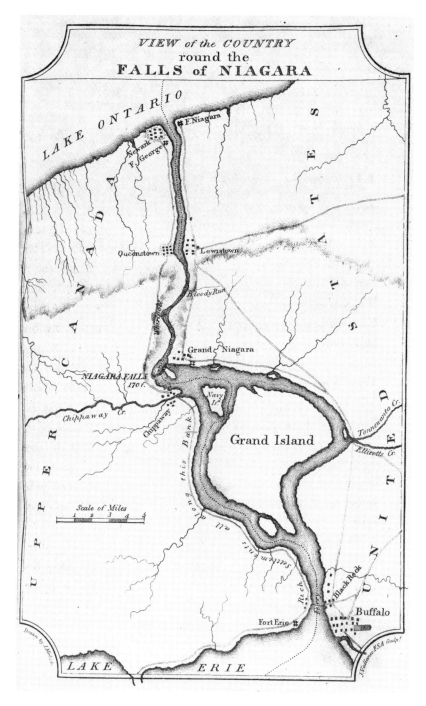

A circa 1812 map of the Niagara River including Navy Island by John Melish. *David Rumsey Map Collection.*

Engraving of an 1842 print by William Henry Bartlett showing Navy Island from the Canadian side.

> *the privates; and the officers alone were entrusted with them. Sutherland brought out a flag, on which was inscribed the word "Liberty" and two stars, to designate the Upper and Lower Province.*

As the news of the occupation spread, small groups of Canadian refugees and American volunteers journeyed to Navy Island. The ranks swelled. Those who did not come to fight lent a hand. Surgeons came to tend to the wounded and the sick. Engineers helped design fortifications. Former military officers advised on defense. Recruits brought cannons stolen from New York State arsenals. Brigadier General Sutherland arrived with a company.

The legality of preparing for a war on Canada was debatable. The United States Neutrality Act forbade anyone from attacking another country at peace with America. Planning for war and gathering weapons fell into a gray area until Washington toughened the law in 1838. Certainly, no one tried to stop the waves of Patriots marching through Buffalo to the Schlosser Harbor on the Niagara River. Once on Navy Island, the Patriots stood beyond the reach of American law until they returned.

Navy Island's north side boasts high banks with a good view of mainland Canada. The Patriots immediately dug in their artillery there and commenced bombarding the Canadian shore.

Van Rensselaer strutted about the island, a cutlass in one hand and brandy in the other. As weeks passed, his drunkenness was obvious and his cowardice suspected. Wood later stated, "Sutherland was in a state of great terror while he was on the island; he could not sleep and was continually calling the men to arms."

Men sought action but found boredom and only crude huts for shelter from the cold and snow. Even as new recruits joined the island's defenders, a steady stream of deserters departed for home. At its peak, the island's Patriot force numbered approximately six hundred, almost equally Canadian and American.

Colonel MacNab arrived to defend the Niagara frontier within days of the occupation. Militia, volunteers and Native warriors joined MacNab and swelled his force to over two thousand. The colonel set up his own artillery and fired on the island, with little effect. Accounts say weeks of bombardment killed one Patriot and wounded several others.

An appendix in Edwin Guillet's book on the Patriot War lists the names of 370 men who joined the rebel forces on Navy Island. He based the list on papers belonging to Charles Lindsey, Mackenzie's biographer. The names of known participants, such as Samuel Wood and Robert Marsh, are not included, indicating that the list is incomplete.

A circa 1896 painting of Sir Allan Napier MacNab by Sir Edmund Wyly Grier based on an existing photograph, circa 1860. *Toronto Public Library.*

In his memoirs, Robert Marsh described being in a trench through a nine-day British bombardment of the rebel stronghold. The rebels viewed the intense but mostly fruitless military exercise as humorous and worth a bit of sarcasm. Marsh wrote:

They were very lavish with Her Gracious Majesty's powder and balls. I recollect a man standing behind the breastwork where were four of us sitting as the balls were whistling through the trees. "Well," says he, "if this is the way to kill the timber on this island, it is certainly a very expensive way, as well as somewhat comical; I should think it would be cheaper to come over with axes."

The opposing forces reached a stalemate. If MacNab had patiently held his ground, as his orders from Bond Head stated, the Patriot War may have fizzled out that winter. But Colonel MacNab, arrogant by nature and angered by the Patriot cannon fire, sanctioned a military action that did more to boost support for the conflict than any of Mackenzie's or Dr. Duncombe's fiery speeches.

At about 11:00 p.m. on December 29, 1837, Captain Andrew Drew, forty-five, acting on MacNab's orders, rowed across the icy river in darkness with sixty armed militia in small boats and boarded the Patriot's rented supply ship, the *Caroline*, at Schlosser (near present-day Niagara Falls, New York). Ten crew men and about twenty-three others, probably Patriot recruits, slept on the steamer.

This painting depicts the widely published but incorrect demise of the *Caroline*. It is one of several artistic creations that show the ship plunging intact over Niagara Falls with people on board. *Library of Congress.*

American accounts state that only the sentry carried a musket. Some British accounts insist that several of "the pirates" were armed and fired at their men, though Captain Drew's later deposition stated that only one occupant of the ship fired a weapon. What no one disputes is that the British crossed the border to attack an American ship in U.S. waters.

Samuel Wood later stated under oath that General Van Rensselaer had warned Captain Appleby not to moor the steamship on the mainland. The general believed British spies had reconnoitered Schlosser Harbor. Appleby disobeyed, citing a problem with his boilers.

Drew's raiders stormed the ship and shot a black American sailor named Amos Durfee in the back of his head. He became the war's first American casualty—but not the last.

Drew's men put Durfee's body on the dock, started fires fore and aft on the *Caroline* and towed the ship into the current to prevent damage to the wharf. The blazing craft grounded on rocks and broke apart, and its pieces plummeted over the falls.

In sworn depositions on December 30, 1837, and February 2, 1838, the *Caroline*'s captain, Gilman Appleby, stated that after the attack, he could not account for ten men who had were on board: "The ten individuals, besides the said Amos Durfee, who are still missing, this deponent has no doubt were either murdered upon the said boat or found a watery grave in the cataract of the Niagara Falls."

Newspapers reported the fanciful stories by Captain Appleby and others, including fibs that women and children perished as the *Caroline* plunged over the falls. Those tales took months to quash. In the end, facts showed that only Durfee died in the attack. Captain Appleby and two others received minor wounds.

Americans saw the British attack on an American ship in a U.S. port as an assault on their sovereignty. The burning of the *Caroline* incensed Americans along the border. In numerous cities and towns, prominent men held public meetings to denounce the insult. More men and cannon (twenty-four in all) arrived on Navy Island.

In his 1890 memoirs, Samuel Alanson Lane, an Ohio sheriff, newspaperman and member of the Patriots, related several resolutions adopted by prominent members of the Akron, Ohio community at a meeting held on January 6, 1838. It was typical of civic reaction along the border.

Resolved: That as true friends of the great cause of liberty, as good and worthy citizens of the United States, and as patriots, we cannot remain silent when oppression stretches forth her hand to smite her victim; stand unconcerned when we see our shores invaded by the armed bands of the hostile slaves of despots whose tender mercies are cruelty and death; nor will we remain idle and senseless when our country calls us to her defense.

Resolved: That the attack, massacre, and destruction of the steamboat Caroline, *by British troops, when lying in an American port, is an insult upon the American flag and an outrage too flagrant to be brooked by a free and independent people.*

The Patriots, as well as similar organizations that formed later, attracted a diverse membership that brought all classes of society—the working class and the wealthy—together in the common cause. The movement also attracted ne'er-do-wells, as Lane discovered when he enlisted in the Patriots:

The writer, on being initiated into the order, at the instance of one of the most highly respected and enterprising merchants of Akron, found himself in the presence of and cheek-by-jowl with the most notorious counterfeiter of his time and several well-known gamblers, together with village councilmen, justices of the peace, lawyers, doctors, merchants, manufacturers, etc.

But while a large proportion of the criminal and dissolute classes identified themselves with the Patriot movement, the great majority of the members of these lodges were from the more reputable classes of society, who, heartily sympathizing with their believed to be oppressed and suffering neighbors, were willing to aid them to the extent of their pecuniary ability, and some of them with their good right arms, and military prowess, if necessary, to accomplish their object.

While President Martin Van Buren accepted a lame apology from the colony and shrugged off the incident, U.S. citizens sent money and ammunition to Patriot organizations. American volunteers soon outnumbered Canadians in the Patriot army on Navy Island. Burning the *Caroline* was a rash military act. It mutated a bungled revolt into a yearlong undeclared border war that cost the English treasury millions of dollars.

The *Caroline* affair rekindled a dying conflict. For his part in it, Colonel MacNab received a knighthood.

ROBERT MARSH

Born in New York State in 1812, Robert Marsh was living in Chippawa, Upper Canada, across from Navy Island when Mackenzie and Van Rensselaer occupied it. The village, Marsh later wrote, filled with Canada's diverse defenders "about 2,000 regulars, Indians and Negroes."

Late in December 1837, Marsh said a friend told him that the British planned to attack and sink the steamer *Caroline*. Marsh discounted the news, believing an unarmed American ship would never be attacked in an American port. A day later, he witnessed the *Caroline*'s demise. Like so many Americans, the assault on U.S. sovereignty changed him from a concerned bystander to a participant.

Marsh evaded the British sentries patrolling the river's shore, crossed to Navy Island via Grand Island and joined Mackenzie's rebels on January 1, 1838.

Marsh left the island on January 13, 1838, when the rebel army evacuated. A week later, he joined other veterans in a five-day walk through the winter countryside to Sandusky, Ohio, where he prepared for further battles.

HENRY S. HANDY

In Michigan in late 1837, Henry S. Handy, thirty-three, like Sutherland, felt certain that Canadian colonists would soon rebel, and he prepared for it.

Born and educated in Pompey, New York, Handy was drawn early into frontier opportunities and politics. He settled in Indiana. His name appears on the list of admitted attorneys in Jackson County, Indiana, in April 1827. That same year, he started a newspaper in Salem, *The Annotator* (it folded in 1828), and married Laura W. Bellows (who divorced him in 1843).

Handy was an early supporter of Andrew Jackson. Handy used his newspaper as a pulpit for Jackson and served as the state chairman of his election committee. Jackson, a master of patronage, rewarded Handy on multiple occasions, starting with the job of the Salem, Indiana postmaster shortly after Jackson's victory. Handy later served in the Pension Bureau of the War Department in Washington, D.C.

In 1833, Jackson appointed Handy as assistant superintendent of Chicago Harbor, where he managed construction of the new facility with distinction while also serving on a committee overseeing the creation of a regional railway. His efforts earned him inclusion in an 1833 book listing five hundred influential Chicagoans. (The book mistakenly lists him as Henry T. Handy.) That year also saw him admitted to practice at the bar of the U.S. Supreme Court.

With the end of Jackson's presidency early in 1837, Handy, still a young man, seemed to need a new challenge. The talk of possible rebellion in Canada caught his attention.

To investigate the rumors, Handy visited Toronto in the fall of 1837 accompanied by Orange Butler, then of the Michigan House of Representatives. They met with reform leader Marshall Bidwell and a fellow named Dufort, a messenger from Lower Canada's rebel leader, Louis-Joseph Papineau. The meetings confirmed Handy's analysis—both colonies verged on rebellion. He and Butler returned to Detroit, where they formed a "war council" of influential citizens. Handy became top general. His list of senior officers included an eclectic mix of idealists and oddballs, including brigadier generals cut from such different cloth that they ended up battling each other.

EDWARD ALEXANDER THELLER

Dr. Edward Alexander Theller was born in Coleraine, Ireland, in 1804. As a young man, Theller taught school in Belfast. He arrived in Montreal in 1826. Though there less than a year, he recognized the deep animosity the French-speaking populace had for the English government—a feeling any Irishman understood.

Theller moved to Vermont and married Ann Wilson in Burlington in 1827, and the couple had five children. Restless and reckless by nature, he drifted through several states, not staying long. He settled in Detroit in 1836. There he practiced medicine and ran an apothecary.

An Irish rebel by inclination and a supporter of underdogs by nature, Dr. Theller, thirty-three, believed it was every American's duty to assist the Canadian rebels, and he said so at numerous public meetings. He joined the Patriot army in December 1837 just days after the defeat of Mackenzie's rebels near Toronto. General Handy appointed him as a brigadier general to head a brigade of Irish and French Canadians, though no such troops existed then or later.

ELIJAH JACKSON ROBERTS

The family of Connecticut-born Elijah Jackson Roberts moved to New York State shortly after his birth in 1802. When the War of 1812 broke out, ten-year-old Roberts joined the entourage of General Erastus Root as a junior orderly. At the war's end, young Roberts studied law in Root's office. At eighteen, he began working on the first of many New York newspapers, the *Western Courier* (1820–21). At twenty, Roberts married a girl of fifteen, Lydia Smith. He continued as an editor or owner of a string of newspapers. In 1829–30, he was editor of the *Craftsman*, a pro-Mason paper in Rochester that battled several anti-Mason papers. (It is possible he tangled editorially at some point with Thomas Jefferson Sutherland.)

While historical accounts describe Roberts as gentle and well mannered, he did have a temper. In 1828, Roberts became embroiled in a very public spat with Mordecai Manuel Noah, a vocal defender of Jews and their rights in America. The latter accused Roberts of assault on the steps of a theater. Roberts and Noah were formerly partners in the New York *National Advocate*, but they did not get along. In 1826, both partners appeared as witnesses for Erastus Root, then lieutenant governor of New York, in a libel case. Root sued the New York owners of the *American* newspaper for saying that he was intoxicated while carrying out his duties. Noah's defense testimony was half-hearted. On the stand, Elijah defended his old mentor Root and cast doubt on the credibility of Noah. (Root won his suit.) What actually precipitated the donnybrook two years later is not recorded, but anti-Semitism seems to be a factor.

Roberts moved his family to Detroit in 1833 and began practicing law. He became well known for his abilities, his distinguished good looks and his principles. In 1837, General Handy recruited Roberts, thirty-five, as a brigadier general in his army of liberation.

HUGH BRADY

The greatest impediment to rebel success during the Patriot War in the west was an aging American general named Hugh Brady. Born in Standingstone, Pennsylvania, in 1768, he began his army career in 1792. He fought at the Battle of Lundy's Lane in the War of 1812 (severely wounded, he sat out the rest of that conflict). In 1837, Brady was given command of Military

Photograph of General Hugh Brady taken between 1844 and 1851. *Library of Congress.*

Department No. 7, headquartered in Detroit. His territory covered Michigan and Ohio—all of General Handy's war territory.

While the United States did have a neutrality law, its ambiguous wording left it open to interpretation. For most of the conflict, American authorities in New York and Vermont behaved as if they believed that the act could be enforced only after an attack occurred—planning an attack was legal. Huge stockpiles of weapons accumulated in New York unmolested by the authorities.

General Brady formed a stricter interpretation. He decided to prevent attacks by confiscating the means of war at every opportunity. The western Patriot War would have been a bloodier affair without his intervention.

NAVY ISLAND ABANDONED

The opposing forces at Navy Island continued to bombard each other for two weeks following the *Caroline* affair. Patriot fighters steadily deserted the island due to cold and boredom. On January 13, 1838, Van Rensselaer abandoned Navy Island and withdrew his men to Buffalo. That did not end the conflict or Van Rensselaer's command of operations. He'd already sent General Sutherland to take charge of the Patriots' western front.

On Van Rensselaer's orders, Patriots moved the cannon, arms and ammunition stored on Navy Island to the steamer *Barcelona*. The general wanted them shipped to Lake Erie for use in other campaigns. On learning the weapons were about to be shipped, Captain Drew readied two gunboats to intercept the steamer. Reports say at least one anchored in American waters. American general Winfield Scott decided to prevent any further assaults on United States sovereignty. He placed cannon along the shore and threatened to blow Drew out of the water if he attacked another American ship. Drew's ships withdrew, and the *Barcelona* sailed on.

Several historical accounts state that the early winter of 1837–38 was far milder than normal. Lakes Ontario and Erie, which in the nineteenth century were ice covered by December, stayed navigable throughout December and into early January. Then a cold snap froze both lakes solid.

A circa 1860 sketch of General Winfield Scott by Benson Lossing in his 1869 book *Pictorial Field-Book of the War of 1812.*

Van Rensselaer returned to the Eagle Tavern in Buffalo to confer with other Patriot leaders about the 1838 campaign. The fighting was far from over.

Chapter 4

Western Patriots Launch First Invasion:
January 1838

G eneral Henry S. Handy and his war council began to gather troops and weapons in reaction to the Upper Canada rebellion in early December 1837.

Between December 23, 1837, and January 8, 1838, General Handy's troops stole seven hundred rifles and muskets plus ammunition from state jails and arsenals.

On New Year's Day 1838, General Handy held a public meeting to raise money and arms. A Detroit theater owner donated several days' proceeds to General Handy's new Patriot Army of the Northwest. His cause had popular support, including from Michigan's first governor, Stevens Thomson Mason (October 27, 1811–January 4, 1843), who appears to have been a member of the Patriots. He was then and still is the youngest state governor in U.S. history.

To attack Canada, General Handy needed ships. To that purpose, his men stole or commandeered the steamboat *McComb* to use as a troop carrier. Before the steamer could transport a single soldier, General Hugh Brady had it seized. General Handy arranged for another steamer. General Brady took that one, too.

The Patriots also took over the schooner *Anne* on January 6, 1838, to ship their munitions and provisions. The ship had no sails onboard, so General Brady's men did not guard it.

To outwit General Brady, General Handy gave Major General James Wilson a set of orders: march the troops under cover of night to Gibraltar at the mouth of the Detroit River, across from Fort Malden, Upper Canada; tow the *Anne* down the river with yawls; and secure sails for the ship. Wilson succeeded and reached his destination early on January 5. Brigadier General Roberts came to Gibraltar to take command of the seven hundred men there.

Fort Malden was a small fort built after the War of 1812 with earthen walls surrounded by a ditch. Wooden pickets topped the walls, most of them rotten and tilting by late 1837.

General Handy accompanied other troops to Peach Island upstream from Detroit opposite Windsor, Upper Canada. He planned to have

Portrait of Mason T. Stevens. *Michigan State Archives.*

This scale model in the Fort Malden Museum shows the rebuilt fort as it appeared at the end of 1838. The two largest buildings (numbers 6 and 9) were new barracks not present in early 1838. *Photo by the author.*

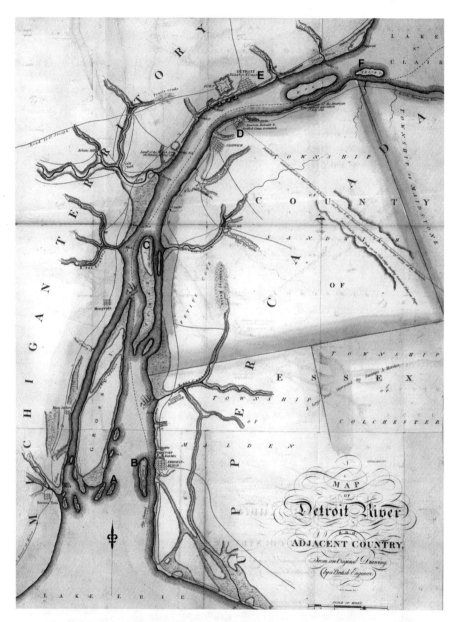

Annotated map of the Detroit River showing key locations: A. Sugar Island, B. Bois Blanc (Boblo) Island and Amherstburg, C. Fighting Island, D. Windsor, E. Detroit and F. Peach Island. Original by John Melish, circa 1813. *David Rumsey Map Collection.*

General Roberts occupy Canada's Bois Blanc Island across from Fort Malden. Bois Blanc Island, now commonly called Boblo Island, is two and a half miles long and lies one thousand feet from the town of Amherstberg, Ontario.

General Roberts's orders were to command all Canadian defenses to surrender on January 9 and then attack the fort if they refused. On the same day, General Handy intended to land troops north of Windsor. The two attacks would split the limited defenses that Upper Canada had available in the region.

There were no British regular troops in the Western District at that time. Lieutenant Governor Francis Bond Head, in distant Toronto, believed no threat existed along the Detroit River. A few hundred volunteer militiamen, infantry and cavalry under Colonel Thomas Radcliffe and about one hundred Native warriors composed the entire defense. The defenders had no cannon and limited arms. Mackenzie's occupation of Navy Island had drawn Colonel MacNab's large army to the banks opposite. In the event of an invasion in the west, his army would need three or four days to cover the distance.

In General Handy, the Western District faced a true threat. He represented a competent leader whose army was larger and better equipped. His two-pronged attack plan could have worked if his eastern allies had not interfered at the last minute.

On December 28, 1837, supreme Patriot commander General Rensselaer Van Rensselaer issued the following order:

> *Brig.-Gen. Sutherland will repair with all dispatch to Detroit and its vicinity and promote every arrangement for making a descent upon Canada in favor of the Patriots, as he in his judgment may deem advisable, after consulting with the Canadian and American friends in that quarter.*

On his way west, General Thomas Jefferson Sutherland stopped in Cleveland, Ohio, to rally people to the Patriot cause. By his authority as brigadier general of the Patriot army, he offered each volunteer three hundred acres of Canadian land and $100 in silver by May 1 if they joined him. At least one hundred men enlisted.

On January 7, General Sutherland arrived at Gibraltar on a steamer with his Ohio troops. Not surprisingly, General Handy's senior officers balked when the "easterner" showed up expecting to run the show. General Roberts, whose allegiance rested with General Handy, sent an urgent dispatch to his commanding officer about General Sutherland's arrival and claims.

General Theller sided with General Sutherland, as did the Ohio troops, who had no knowledge of General Handy's organization and believed

General Van Rensselaer's orders ought to be respected. From afar, General Handy, whose command was independent of Van Rensselaer, proposed a compromise: "That if General Sutherland would implicitly obey the orders of the commander in chief [Handy] sent to General Roberts, command should be given to him [Sutherland] until by express I [Handy] could reach the island."

General Sutherland agreed and assumed command of the Gibraltar forces, placing General Theller in charge of the schooner *Anne*.

General Sutherland believed Canadian defenders might be stationed on Bois Blanc Island, so instead of landing his troops there, as General Handy intended, General Sutherland moved them to Sugar Island, safely in American waters.

On the evening of January 8, General Theller commanded the schooner to sail up the channel between Bois Blanc Island and Amherstburg in the

A six-pound cannon protrudes from a gun port aboard a modern schooner replica. *Photo by the author.*

moonlight. When passing the fort, Canadian sentinels hailed the ship. Receiving no answer, the plucky Canadian militia ignored the cannon on the *Anne* and fired muskets at its crew. In response, General Theller had his men fire their six-pound cannon at the sleepy town of Amherstburg. The militia had no cannon with which to reply.

General Roberts lost his temper. He denounced General Theller's cannon fire on the town as a piratical act because no call for surrender preceded it. (In Dr. Theller's memoirs, he claims his ship fired in self-defense to end a fusillade of musket fire that had already wounded two of his crew.)

That same evening, General Theller again sailed the *Anne* between the island and the shore. He later reported that the rickety schooner became unmanageable due to inadequate rigging and a weary crew. It ran aground at the foot of Bois Blanc Island, but the men refloated her. That grounding proved to be an omen.

General Roberts urged his commander to arrest Generals Sutherland and Theller. General Handy did dispatch two colonels in a canoe to arrest the generals the next day, but they turned back in rough weather.

Following a report from General Theller that Bois Blanc Island was deserted, General Sutherland took sixty men by boat and occupied the island and its 1836 lighthouse on January 9. Old blockhouses, remnants of earlier

> One of the colonels in the canoe was a U.S. District Court judge named Ross Wilkins, according to Charles Lindsey. In the following months, Wilkins ironically served as the presiding judge in eight cases in which Patriots, including Generals Sutherland and Theller, were charged with breaching the neutrality law—the same law Wilkins broke that day. Wilkins, backed by sympathetic juries, dismissed each man except for one.

British fortifications on the island, provided some shelter. They hoisted a tri-colored flag, and General Sutherland read a proclamation to the citizens of Upper Canada that no colonist could hear and few ever saw, urging them to accept his force as liberators.

On the morning of January 9, the *Anne* again sailed between the island and the mainland, this time in a heavy shoreward wind. Again, the ship fired cannon at the town.

The local militia fought back. Sharpshooters peppered the schooner with musket and shotgun fire, tearing its rigging to bits and wounding the helmsman. In the confusion of battle, the *Anne* drifted, ran aground at Elliot's Point (downstream from the town) and heeled over, exposing its deck to the

The lighthouse built on Boblo Island in 1836 remains today as a historic site. *Photo by the author.*

militia. Canadian marksmen began picking off anyone on the ship's deck. One crewman died, and many sustained wounds, including General Theller. The entire crew scurried below deck to escape the hail of musket balls and buckshot.

Patriots on the island saw the *Anne*'s plight. Rather than go to the schooner's aid, as his men wanted, General Sutherland ordered a retreat

Sketch of the naval wharf at Fort Malden by Benson Lossing in his book *Pictorial Field-Book of the War of 1812*. In the background on the left is Elliot Point, where the *Anne* ran aground. In the back center is the lighthouse on Bois Blanc Island.

to Sugar Island in U.S. waters. He is said to have cried out, "Away to Sugar Island. Fly, fly, fly—all is lost."

Among the troops firing on the *Anne* was Lieutenant William Lewis Baby, twenty-five. Like most able-bodied male colonists, he had trained with the militia as part of his civic duty. When the call to arms came, he shouldered his own shotgun and joined one hundred other volunteers from the Windsor and Chatham areas and hurried to Fort Malden.

> *A company of former American slaves joined in capturing the* Anne. *When the Upper Canada rebellion began, nearly one thousand former slaves volunteered for the militia.*

The Canadian militia, led by Lieutenant Baby, waded to their armpits in the freezing January water. Climbing on the backs of others, they boarded the *Anne* and captured General Theller—easily spotted as the only man in a uniform—and his crew without a fight. Baby found twenty-one men, including one dead and eight wounded. He confiscated the ship's two hundred muskets, ammunition and three cannon, which significantly bolstered the militia arsenal.

General Theller later described the bloody encounter with the Canadian militia:

In 1977, Parks Canada commissioned artist C.H. Forster to re-create several battle scenes from the Patriot War. This one reconstructs the capture of the schooner *Anne* and General Theller. *Courtesy Fort Malden Museum.*

As we neared the town, volley after volley was poured into us with considerable effect, and with more skill than the night before. It was no boys' play now—many of our men were wounded and considerable damage done to the rigging. Captain Davis, who was holding on to the anchor, was shot in the wrist, and from which he afterwards died, and away went the anchor. The enemy aimed with fatal precision at the helmsman, and he fled below, leaving the boat to her own will, and as the down-hauls had been cut away by the shot, the sails could not be managed. Unskilled as mariners, confusion reigned among us, and the schooner drifting with the ice, we were in a few moments aground on the main shore, our deck presenting an inclined front to the irritated and triumphant marksmen of the enemy.

Dodge, Brophy, myself and a few others, determined to sell our lives at as dear a rate as possible, and still hoping that the force on the island would come to our rescue, maintained for a while our position on the deck and with much labor brought our cannon to bear upon the shore. Another volley and a rush to board us. The moon was shining bright, and we were easily seen and marked by their riflemen, while they were concealed behind the fences and the trees of an orchard close at hand. Dodge was wounded in the eye, and fell, as I then thought, dead at my feet; Brophy was soon after disabled by a wound. I received a blow on the head that felled me to the deck and down the hatchway to the hold.

Lieutenant Baby personally carried General Theller to shore. He treated the general and his crew as prisoners of war. His militia companions took great pains to provide the eight wounded shelter and medical care. General Theller spoke well of his treatment immediately upon capture:

Stunned and senseless, I was dragged out by the victors and placed in custody for future disposition. On recovering, I found myself and others in the charge of Lieut. Baby, who protected me from insult, and who was aided in this manly duty by Captain Rudyard and Colonel Radcliff, the latter saying in my hearing that we were prisoners of war, had conducted ourselves like brave men, and must not be abused but be handed over to the proper authorities for judicial treatment.

David Anderson, a former rebel leader from Yarmouth, Upper Canada, died of his wounds at Fort Malden. Another wounded captive, Robert Davis, an author from the London area, died in the summer from his wounds.

Upper Canada had offered a £100 reward for Anderson's capture. The men who stormed the *Anne* shared the reward.

One serious casualty who no one expected to live was William Wallin Dodge, a merchant from Monroe, Michigan. He had taken a shot in the eye.

On January 10, General Handy arrived at Gibraltar and boated with General Roberts to Sugar Island. General Sutherland offered General Handy the command, but he perversely declined. Generals Sutherland and Handy then—amazingly—put the leadership to a vote. Of the seven hundred men, all but two voted for General Handy. General Sutherland departed for Detroit.

On inspecting Sugar Island, General Handy found fewer than sixty muskets fit for use—he'd lost the bulk of his arsenal on the *Anne*. A few days later, he moved all troops and munitions off the island with the aid of a ferry steamer sent by the supportive Michigan governor. With harsh winter weather now upon them, and General Brady watching his every move, General Handy canceled immediate plans for invasion. Thus ended the only real chance for a sustained Patriot success in Upper Canada. In the months ahead, Britain bolstered its defenses in Upper Canada, making a Patriot military success less and less likely. That did not stop the rebels from trying.

JOSIAH HENSON

While most historical accounts of the defense of Amherstburg and the capture of the *Anne* describe the heroics of white militiamen, such as William Baby, the defenders included Natives from a local reserve and an all-black company, with Reverend Josiah Henson, forty-eight, as its leader.

Henson was born into slavery in Maryland. Over the years, he witnessed his father brutalized and all his family, except his mother, sold off. While a slave, he became a Methodist preacher. He escaped along the Underground Railroad to western Upper Canada with his wife and children in October 1830 and became a farm hand. In his autobiography, he gave a brief account of his part in the Upper Canada rebellion:

> *I was appointed a captain to the 2ⁿᵈ Essex Company of Coloured Volunteers. Though I could not shoulder a musket* [because of his religion], *I could carry a sword. My company held Fort Malden from Christmas till the following May, and also took the schooner* Anne *and captured all it carried, which were three hundred arms, two cannons, musketry, and provisions for the*

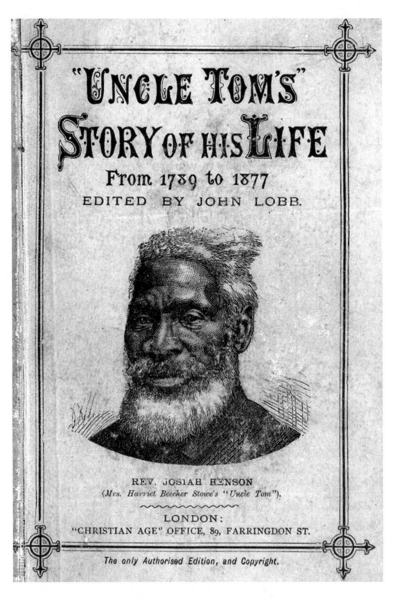

"UNCLE TOM'S" STORY OF HIS LIFE

From 1789 to 1877

EDITED BY JOHN LOBB.

REV. JOSIAH HENSON
(Mrs. Harriet Beecher Stowe's "Uncle Tom").

LONDON:
"CHRISTIAN AGE" OFFICE, 89, FARRINGDON ST.

The only Authorised Edition, and Copyright.

Image of Josiah Henson on the cover of his autobiography.

rebel troops. This was a fierce and gallant action, and it did much towards breaking up the rebel party, for they could not obtain provisions while we held the fort, which we continued to do till we were relieved by the colonel of the 44th Regiment from England. The coloured men were willing to help defend the government that had given them a home when they had fled from slavery.

Henson did serve with the Second Essex Company on January 10, 1838, but his captaincy is likely an autobiographical embellishment. Typically, white officers commanded black companies in that era.

JOHN PRINCE

COL. JOHN PRINCE.

Sketch of Colonel John Prince in later life, from William Baby's memoirs.

No defender of the Western District of Upper Canada in 1838 stands out as prominently as Colonel John Prince—more for his histrionics than heroism.

Prince was born in England in 1796. He became a lieutenant at age seventeen and a practicing lawyer at twenty-five. In 1833, he moved his family to Upper Canada and settled at Sandwich (now part of present-day Windsor, Ontario). He bought property for farming and worked as a lawyer. As one of the few educated men in the young colony, he did well. He became a magistrate in July 1835. He was elected to the Legislative Assembly in 1836 and pushed forward several progressive bills. He became a colonel in the Essex County militia in 1837.

Prince became notorious for his ill temper and poor treatment of captured rebels.

ANNE PRISONERS SENT TO JAIL

The day after the militia captured the *Anne*, the gentle treatment of the prisoners ended. Colonel John Prince stormed into the farmhouse where Lieutenant Baby housed his captives. The colonel walked up to the sleeping General Theller, kicked him in the ribs and shouted, "Get up you damned piratical scoundrel."

General Theller later described Prince as "armed to the teeth"—sword, double-barreled gun, brace of pistols, tomahawk—and noted that "his whole appearance betokened triumphant malignity and determined vengeance."

In his memoirs, William Baby excused the colonel's temper that day:

> Colonel Prince's treatment of Theller would appear to be harsh, cruel, and unofficer-like, but when it is considered that the inhabitants along the whole frontier...were in a constant state of fear and trembling, expecting that every moment their houses would be fired and they murdered by these piratical ruffians...Prince well knew the characters he had to deal with, and he treated them as they well deserved.

Colonel Prince ordered Lieutenant Baby to rope all but the most gravely wounded prisoners together and take them to the guard house in Amherstburg. The prisoners rode in the back of an open cart in the dreary winter to a local dungeon, as General Theller described it. From there, they were carted to the Toronto jail to await trial.

Sutherland Founders Further

Just days after botching General Handy's invasion, Sutherland further sullied his reputation as a competent Patriot commander. By prior arrangement, a troop of sympathetic U.S. militia in Detroit purposely left three hundred weapons unguarded for General Handy's men to replenish those they lost. However, General Sutherland made off with the weapons instead and hid them poorly. They were retaken by American authorities and locked up. General Brady restricted the supply of weapons to the militia for months afterward, thus depriving General Handy of his best source.

On January 13, 1838, authorities arrested General Sutherland in Detroit for violating American neutrality laws. He came before Judge Ross Wilkins, the man once sent by General Handy to arrest him. Juries in Michigan and Ohio showed great reluctance to convict Patriots of any rank—the court acquitted Sutherland.

Chapter 5

Fighting Island Occupied: February 1838

Following the withdrawal of Patriots from Navy Island in January 1838, General Rensselaer Van Rensselaer recruited a new set of officers. Together, they planned simultaneous raids on the eastern and western fronts for February 22, George Washington's birthday. General Van Rensselaer took charge of (and bungled) the eastern raid on Kingston and Gananoque along the St. Lawrence River. He tasked rebel newcomer General Donald McLeod with the western campaign. (*The Patriot War Along the New York-Canada Border* details General Van Rensselaer's botched assault.)

DONALD MCLEOD

Donald McLeod came to the Patriot cause at age fifty-nine with more war experience than any other Patriot officer. Born in Scotland in 1779, he joined the British navy in 1803 and switched to the infantry in 1808. He fought against Napoleon, including at Waterloo. As a sergeant in the War of 1812, he served at Queenston Heights, Lundy's Lane and Crysler's Farm—three pivotal victories for colonial Canada.

McLeod retired from the army and settled in Prescott, Upper Canada, where he continued his life as a loyal citizen. He became a militia major, a schoolteacher and a newspaper publisher who championed political reform. In the days following the rebel rout at Toronto in December

1837, a "Tory mob," as McLeod put it, trashed his printing office as a warning. Angry at his mistreatment, McLeod fled to Buffalo and joined General Van Rensselaer's army.

March to Battle

General McLeod and hundreds of Navy Island veterans began the long, wintry march from Buffalo to eastern Michigan on January 18, 1838. With him were many Navy Island veterans, including John Vreeland, H.C. Seward, Lester Hoadley, Benjamin Wait, Benjamin Lett, Robert Marsh and Samuel Wood.

On the second day, U.S. colonel William Jenkins Worth and his company of troops confiscated all General McLeod's weapons and supplies to enforce the U.S. neutrality law.

General McLeod continued on, his army fed and housed by sympathetic country residents. At Sandusky, Ohio, he paused to confer with other Patriot officers. They decided to split the army, then about one thousand, with half staying and half leaving with General McLeod on February 18.

In a letter to his wife, McLeod spoke of his first Patriot mission:

> I am at the head of 500 as brave men as ever handled a gun. I shall shortly be in Canada with them to pay the Tories a visit. Kiss each of the children for me. Give my respects to all true reformers. I have now traveled upwards of 500 miles on the American side. The Citizens are the most generous and noble-hearted people the world can produce. If we fail in setting Canada free, it will not be their fault; money, men and other means they have given with cheerful hearts. In fact, their kindness will compel us to fight and conquer, whether or not. Farewell my Dear wife for the present. You shall hear from me every week. Your last injunction to me was never to fill a Coward's Grave. Depend upon it, my loving, brave and heroic wife.

The wintry march remained difficult. One of the combatants with General McLeod, Robert McFarlan, then just eighteen, wrote about the long march in an 1885 letter to the *Detroit Free Press*:

> The greatest difficulty they had to encounter was to find a place in which to sleep, there being no trouble in procuring enough to eat. A bed was

a great luxury, and but few were enabled to enjoy one; in fact, almost the entire squad were obliged to lie upon bar-room floors and in other uncomfortable places.

People of this day often wonder how so large a company of men could have been kept together under such adverse and depressing circumstances. Well, I know of no other incentive except their devotion to the cause, a promise of good pay, and that at the termination of the war, if successful, each man was to receive 160 acres of land anywhere in the Province of Upper Canada.

Samuel Wood gave another, more practical reason why the Patriots put up with the harsh conditions, writing, "I believe that many would have abandoned the Patriot cause, but we were in the midst of winter and could not get a day's work, and we had more chance of relief as Patriots than in a private capacity."

Patriot recruits in Detroit heard of the approaching army and expected a battle. On February 23, men took over the steamer *Erie*, loaded it with war supplies and sailed from Detroit. It stopped to pick up fighters waiting at the Rising Sun Tavern in Springwells south of Detroit. Those troops boarded the steamer and then continued to join General McLeod.

Another thirty Patriots, including Robert McFarlan, assembled in Detroit's Eagle Tavern that same evening to listen to General Sutherland urge them on to glory. Like its namesake in Buffalo, this tavern was the unofficial headquarters of the Patriot forces. McFarlan relates what happened next:

Next morning, after a scanty breakfast, we were again mustered into line and marched to Springwells, near where [Fort Wayne] now is, where we remained for dinner. Here Gen. Sutherland assured us that, without doubt, a full supply of arms and ammunition would be furnished on our arrival opposite Fighting Island, whither we were trending.

With some considerable enthusiasm, we again took up our line of march, and upon the arrival at the place designated, you may well imagine our disappointment in finding but few guns, and those of very inferior quality, among the rest a six-pound cannon, unmounted. The time having arrived for our march to the island, the commissary stores, consisting of a barrel of salt pork and large dry-goods box of bread, accompanied by the unmounted cannon, were placed upon a sled and drawn across the American channel by the men. The "Patriots" reached the island about 10 o'clock in the evening.

Colonel John Vreeland was in charge of Patriot weapons. He promised to have ample supplies available for the attack on Fighting Island. He did not deliver. He secreted the weapons away and did his best to evade various Patriot officers sent to fetch the weapons. History suggests that he was off his rocker: whenever he was out of sight of General McLeod, he pretended to be the Patriot army commander-in-chief. Using that title, he ran up a significant bill at an inn entertaining himself and officers and left the tab for the Patriot paymaster to deal with.

Dr. Duncombe, recently arrived in America, met with General McLeod. Hearing about his lack of weapons, the rebel doctor tried his best to find Colonel Vreeland and the weapons and, after failing that, journeyed to Detroit to make an appeal for donated weapons. (Some sources indicate that Vreeland sold the weapons and pocketed the money, while others state that he turned the guns, twenty-eight hundred in number, over to U.S. authorities.)

News came to General McLeod that General Brady's men were on their way to intercept his troops. He ordered the rebel army to cross the ice to the Canadian island beyond General Brady's reach.

When General McLeod's army crossed to Fighting Island on February 24, the entire army had just twelve working muskets. Dr. Duncombe arrived after dark with thirty-five more. That still left most of General McLeod's army unarmed.

The rebels had one six-pound cannon stolen from Dearborn, Michigan, after a July 4 celebration months earlier. It had no carriage, so the men mounted it on a large wooden dry-goods box. On the night of February 24, the Patriots set up defenses and prepared their ammunition.

By this point in the Patriot War, the small and under-provisioned local militia that General Handy first faced in January 1838 had been bolstered by impressive numbers of weapons, plus regular troops commanded by seasoned officers: Colonel James Lewis Basden of the Twenty-first Regiment, Lieutenant Colonel John Maitland (recently arrived after helping to crush the rebellion in Lower Canada) with companies of the Thirty-second and Eighty-third Regiments, Major Henry Dive Townsend of the Twenty-fourth Regiment and Captain George Mark Glasgow of the Royal Artillery. Upper Canada and Britain now took the western threat seriously.

General McLeod had no idea of his enemy's true strength, and unbeknownst to him, the British knew in advance of his occupation of Fighting Island. General Brady had earlier sent a message to Colonel Basden, an officer he knew as an opponent during the War of 1812, informing him of the raid on the colony. Basden answered back that he'd drive the brigands

This 1977 painting by C.H. Forster reconstructs the Battle of Fighting Island. *Courtesy Fort Malden Museum.*

off, follow them into America and shoot everyone. That reply riled the old American general. In response, General Brady had his men plant red flags on the river ice to mark the boundary and reportedly told his eight hundred troops that "if a British officer or soldier in arms crosses inside of our lines, I charge you all to beat them back, to capture and to kill them, if it be necessary to protect our sovereignty and to guard our soil against the impress of a British soldier's foot." His men did not have cause to execute that order.

Under command of Major Townsend, five hundred well-armed British regulars and militia, including Lieutenant William Baby and his company, prepared to cross the ice to meet General McLeod's rebels on the morning of February 25, 1838. Captain Glasgow's three cannons opened fire with loads of grapeshot. After a series of barrages, Townsend's troops pressed forward.

The Patriots discharged a few rounds from their muskets and two or three from their cannon (which flopped into the snow each time). Outnumbered and outgunned, General McLeod wisely ordered a retreat.

Robert McFarlan related without undue drama the brief battle in his 1885 letter to the *Detroit Free Press*:

The British troops were marched down the river in fine order, and when opposite their foe, filed to the right and came straight for us, across the ice. When they were thought to be within range of our cannon…the order was given to fire, which was done by a soldier touching it off with a firebrand. The cannon was kicked off the box, and immediately picked up again by a couple of stalwart men, replaced and reloaded with grape.

In the meantime, the British brought their battery, which they had with them, into requisition, and we were soon forcibly reminded that they meant business. Those armed with rifles were now ordered to open fire, which they did with some little effect, as the column of the enemy recoiled for a moment but soon regained order and proceeded toward us. Their battery in the meantime kept up a steady fire, which began to make it very uncomfortable for our men, and the order was given to fall back, which was executed in good order, until they came to some haystacks, where they made another stand, for a few minutes only, and after a few more rounds by our riflemen, a general retreat was made to the American shore.

While McFarlan's account is largely accurate, his 1885 letter insisted that Thomas Jefferson Sutherland commanded the army on Fighting Island, when it was clearly General McLeod who ran the show. Sutherland remained in Detroit extolling men to join the cause.

William Baby told the story from the colonists' perspective:

Captain Glasgow, with three pieces of artillery, had taken up a position commanding a fair sweep of the island, which was covered with a thick growth of burr oaks with their dried leaves still upon them. He opened a fire of grape shot upon the invaders, who were sitting around their camp fires, and such was the effect that before we had time to cross over to the island, not a soul was to be seen.

Robert Marsh, in his memoirs, claimed to be part of the Pelee Island raid that occurred a few days later. But his single bravado-filled paragraph on the subject actually described Fighting Island. He had confused the two engagements after so many years.

Lieutenant Baby and his Kent militia took the captured Patriot cannon home to Chatham. (It now sits in front of the Chatham-Kent Museum.)

Five Patriots received wounds and were carried to the American shore. General McLeod was knocked on the head by a branch torn off a tree by cannon fire. The British reported no casualties.

Taken by sleigh to hotels in Detroit, all wounded Patriots were tended by Dr. George B. Russell, according to historian Robert B. Ross, who "amputated several arms that had been mangled by British grape shot."

General Brady's men waited to capture the fleeing raiders. McFarlan related that they were arrested, marched to Detroit and released a few days later. General McLeod fled in disguise, even wearing women's clothes for a time, but U.S. soldiers caught him. A sympathetic jury later acquitted him.

Benjamin Lett

One of the Patriot fighters who helped carry wounded comrades off Fighting Island was Benjamin Lett, a rebel lieutenant at that engagement and a veteran of Navy Island. Lett evaded General Brady's troops after the retreat and hurried to Sandusky, where he joined an invasion force preparing to march on Pelee Island.

Lett, twenty-five, was born in Ireland in 1813. His family immigrated to Lower Canada in 1819 and settled northwest of Montreal. In 1824, his father died. In 1833, his mother relocated her seven children to a farm in Upper Canada east of Toronto.

Benjamin Lett took up the reform banner but did not start out as a rebel. The brutality of loyalist gangs in Upper Canada in the days following Mackenzie's uprising warped him. Lett, invited to join them, refused and was in turn set upon. Legend has it—and it may be apocryphal—that Lett's hatred for the Canadian establishment solidified into rage when loyalists shot one of his brothers and sexually abused a sister.

Sources described Lett as five feet, eleven inches tall and slim with sandy hair and whiskers. He had a ruddy and freckled face, light skin, penetrating light blue eyes and large and muscular hands with long fingers.

Lett would later become one of the most wanted men in colonial Canada. Throughout the Patriot War, the majority of Patriot raiders followed rules of engagement on par with the British; that is, they generally behaved as soldiers and not murderers. While the colonial government called them pirates and brigands, the rebels were no more or less prone to abuses on the battlefield than the Upper Canadians. The one notable exception was Lett. He evolved from a soldier into an assassin and terrorist bomber. (*The Patriot War Along the New York-Canada Border* describes Lett's misadventures in more detail.)

ERIE ICE ESCAPADE

The American-based Patriot commanders did not sanction every raid on Upper Canada. Exuberant groups of men staged freelance raids between 1838 and 1841. The first of these—and the only one with comedic overtones—occurred in February 1838 (some sources say March) not far from Buffalo, New York.

Thirty to forty men established a camp on the Lake Erie ice close to the border. For shelter, they built wooden shanties with beds made of hemlock boughs. They intended to invade an uninhabited stretch of Upper Canada at night, once their expected reinforcements arrived. To guide their way in the dark, they had embedded a row of hemlock boughs in the ice all the way to the Canadian shore. The men had few rifles, the majority being armed with homemade pikes.

An American militia company on patrol by sleigh to enforce the neutrality law found the camp. They arrested the men and burned their shanties.

While this Lake Erie escapade did no harm to the cause, later freelance raids backfired.

Chapter 6

Pelee Island Overrun: March 1838

The men who General Donald McLeod left behind in Sandusky, Ohio, on the way to Fighting Island were not idle. Under the command of Colonels H.C. Seward and Edwin D. Bradley, recruits from Canada, Michigan, New York, Ohio and Pennsylvania prepared for their own assault on Upper Canada. Major Lester Hoadley, forty-three, and Captain Henry Van Rensselaer, thirty-one, drilled the men, hoping to inject a level of military discipline.

On February 26, the day after General McLeod's defeat at Fighting Island, Colonels Bradley and Seward stepped off the peninsula on the north side of Sandusky Bay onto the ice of Lake Erie and began the fifteen-mile march to Pelee Island in Canadian waters. Four hundred officers and men followed them that day, including veteran Patriot fighters Benjamin Wait and Benjamin Lett. The army crossed the thick ice pulling sleds of weapons and ammunition. Jagged ice ridges slowed their travel.

Upon arrival, they found the ten-thousand-acre island deserted. Its few residents fled in advance to warn the Canadian military. The invaders brought limited food supplies because the Patriot leaders planned to take all they needed from the island residents. And they did. The occupiers stripped the island bare of food stores and livestock, damaged buildings and looted anything they could carry. When the men weren't running amok, Captain Van Rensselaer used his previous army experience to set up drills in an attempt to make the men better soldiers.

The occupying army may have numbered as many as one thousand at some point. Curious spectators crossed over to the island in sleighs from

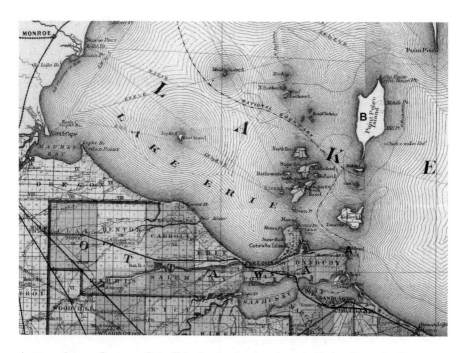

Annotated map of western Lake Erie showing key locations: A. Peninsula north of Sandusky, Ohio and B. Pelee Island. Original by Ormando Willis Gray, circa 1872. *David Rumsey Map Collection.*

Sandusky to view the invasion of Canada, often taking Patriot fighters back and forth with them.

What the Patriots expected to accomplish militarily by overrunning isolated Pelee Island is unclear. It gave them no tactical advantage unless as a diversion for an attack elsewhere. General McLeod's later writing suggested that the raids on Fighting Island and Pelee Island were to be simultaneous; however, Colonels Seward and Bradley had to delay their departure due to Colonel John Vreeland.

Though the colonels had a significant number of men, they had far fewer rifles. Once again, the unstable Colonel Vreeland, the so-called master of ordnances, failed to appear. Colonel Bradley later wrote to General McLeod saying that he had just 152 armed men.

A day before the British arrived to recapture Pelee Island, Colonel Seward suggested to his officers that they abandon the island and go home. Patriot scouts had spotted the advance guard of the British force. The majority refused. Colonel Seward resigned his command in favor of Colonel Bradley.

EDWIN BRADLEY

Edwin D. Bradley was born in 1804 in Litchfield, Connecticut, to Major Daniel Bradley, a veteran of the Revolutionary War. Edwin entered the law office of Beers & Sanford at Litchfield, reading law and attending lectures at the law school. Edwin suffered from health problems and felt it best to leave Connecticut. In 1835, he moved to Sandusky, Ohio, to work in agriculture. In 1837, he became a colonel within the ranks of Americans who wanted to liberate Canada.

About the middle of February 1838, Colonel Bradley began collecting an army at Sandusky to cooperate with General McLeod in an invasion of Canada.

LESTER HOADLEY

Lester Hoadley (1794–1838) was raised in Alexandria Bay, New York. He married Sarah Chipmen on March 4, 1818, and they moved to Utica, New York, in 1824. They had nine children. A civil engineer by trade, he was an educated and prosperous man. Like thousands of Americans caught up in the freedom-fighting frenzy of the times—perhaps a holdover from the Texas Revolution in 1836—Hoadley put aside his normal life to enlist in the overthrow of the British in Canada.

Hoadley began his Patriot enlistment as an infantry captain during the occupation of Navy Island. From there, he joined the Patriot army's western division, where he was elected major on January 29, 1838, at a meeting of Patriot officers in Conneault, Ohio. He joined other officers in planning the Pelee Island raid.

UPPER CANADA COUNTERATTACKS

When word of the Pelee Island invasion reached Lieutenant Colonel John Maitland at Fort Malden several days after the occupation began, he sent Captain George Glasgow to determine if the ice was strong enough to transport cannon. The next day, Captain Glasgow returned with an affirmative reply.

Lieutenant Colonel Maitland set out with four companies of the Thirty-second Regiment, one company of the Eighty-third Regiment, twenty-one members of a volunteer cavalry troop, one company of militia, two six-pound cannon under Captain Glasgow and a small party of Natives acting as scouts—about five hundred men in all. Halfway through the forty-mile journey, Lieutenant Colonel Maitland halted the men by the Erie lakeshore for a brief rest. He timed his arrival for dawn on March 3.

He sent Captain George Browne, a veteran of the Battle of Waterloo, with two companies of the Thirty-second Regiment in sleighs and the cavalry troop to the island's south end to prevent a Patriot retreat. Captain Browne spread his ninety infantrymen in a long line—each man one and a half paces apart—facing the island. The twenty-one-man cavalry troop guarded the east flank.

Lieutenant Colonel Maitland arrived at the island's north end, expecting to engage the main Patriot force. Colonel Bradley had witnessed the move by Captain Browne to get behind them. Knowing his army was outgunned, he had no interest in engaging Lieutenant Colonel Maitland's main force, so he marched his men the length of the island to its south end.

This 1977 painting by C.H. Forster reconstructs the Pelee Island battle. *Courtesy Fort Malden Museum.*

When the Patriots broke from the forest cover, Captain Browne's men suddenly faced an estimated five hundred enemy soldiers—all eager to escape the British army bearing down behind them. The Patriots came from the forest in a column and formed into a long line under the direction of Major Hoadley and Captain Van Rensselaer. With only 152 rifles among them, the armed men took the front rank and began firing at the British troops. The unarmed men waited to pick up rifles from fallen comrades.

Captain Browne's men were the first soldiers in Upper Canada to face Patriot fighters who did not flee after the first shot. With Captain Van Rensselaer and Major Hoadley shouting orders and encouragement, the rebels began inflicting clear and persistent damage on the British regulars. The infantry began to drop onto the ice. The cavalry took heavy fire.

The exchange of gunfire lasted twenty to thirty minutes, with the advantage going to the Patriots. Finally, in desperation, Captain Browne ordered his men to fix their bayonets and charge.

William McCormick, who owned most of Pelee Island then, and his son William Jr. fought in the battle with the regulars. The story of the last moments of the battle and the heroism on both sides was handed down through the McCormick family and recorded by historian Robert B. Ross:

> [Henry] *Van Rensselaer, with the courage of his ancient race, led his men fearlessly in this ignoble cause, while Capt. Browne, an old Waterloo veteran, kept steadily advancing. But* [with] *the rapid fire of the Patriots beginning to tell, Capt. Browne shortly gave the command to fire. Then came the command, "Fix bayonets! Charge!"*
>
> *The line of steel at double-quick, with the half cheer, half roar of British troops bore down to the long line of Patriots near the shore. Van Rensselaer, when the word "charge" was given, was heard to shout, "Charge and be damned." Drawing his sword, he cheered his men on. At this moment, a bullet pierced his forehead, and he jumped high in the air and fell dead.*
>
> *When the order to charge was given, young Wm. McCormick seized a musket from a dying soldier. He was a boy of eighteen but a giant in stature, being six feet four inches in height. He led the charge at a run and was shot twice in the clothing, one ball going through his cap and another passing through his pantaloons and vest.*

The rebels held their ground until the advancing men came within twenty yards. The untrained invaders had no experience at close combat. Terrified by the seventeen-inch, three-sided blades rushing toward them, they let off one final volley and scattered in every direction into the forest and over the ice, chased briefly by the cavalry.

Samuel Wood, who was wounded in the battle, gave the following account in a deposition later that year:

> [We] *went towards the ice intending to retreat, but on rising a knoll on the land, we discovered Captain Browne's detachment, in column on the ice; we were halted, and Bradley, Seward, and Van Rensselaer issued their orders that if any man flinched he should be shot. The Colonel said, "When they come to see there are so many of us, they will retreat, and we can get on that way"; we were ordered not to fire upon them until they should commence…and we marched up in line upon the ice; there was some rough ice near the shore, but not sufficient to shelter a man.*
>
> *The soldiers opened a fire, which we returned as well as we could. I found that I had no flint in my gun, and consequently did not fire. I received a ball in my ear which cut off part of it and buried itself in my cheekbone, and another which broke my thigh bone; three other Patriots fell near me, and young Van Rensselaer was killed at the other end of the line; four others were slightly wounded, but they retreated with the rest. Upon the charge of bayonets from the British, none were killed with the bayonet; the Patriot force retreated about 500 yards and then took the ice again and was not pursued. I lay about three hours on the ice, and [was] taken to Amherstburg.*

When Lieutenant Colonel Maitland arrived with the main force, the battle was over. The Thirty-second Regiment suffered four dead that day or who died later: Privates Thomas McCartan, Samuel Holmes, Edwin Miller and Thomas Symonds. Thomas Parish of the St. Thomas volunteer cavalry also perished. Twenty-five other men bore wounds, many severe enough that they were sent back to England as invalids.

Lieutenant Colonel John Maitland (1789–1839) was the third son of James Maitland, eighth Earl of Lauderdale. He caught a cold during the liberation of Pelee Island and died from its complications after a long illness.

Colonel Bradley later reported the Patriot casualties as "one major, one captain and eight privates killed; and one captain and fifteen privates wounded." Among the dead were Major Hoadley and Captain Van Rensselaer.

The British captured eleven, including Samuel Wood. One

man soon died of his wounds. A report on the battle by Lieutenant Colonel Maitland incorrectly stated that Colonel Bradley died.

The number of British casualties at the Battle of Pelee Island shocked Upper Canada. Until then, routing the rebels had been a lark. But this time, trained by Major Hoadley and Captain Van Rensselaer, they had shown an understanding of tactics and discipline—they were the most effective fighting force the Patriots had fielded so far on the eastern and western fronts.

BENJAMIN WAIT

Benjamin Wait, twenty-four, was born in Upper Canada to American immigrant parents. In 1837, he lived west of Niagara Falls, employed as a businessman and schoolteacher. When the Upper Canada rebellion ignited in Toronto in December 1837, Wait joined Dr. Charles Duncombe's uprising near London just as the British dispersed the rebels. Wait fled to the United States, crossing the Niagara River by canoe. He joined William Lyon Mackenzie's army in the occupation of Navy Island with the rank of lieutenant. When the Patriots withdrew from that island, Wait marched with General McLeod to Sandusky and joined Colonels Seward and Bradley in the Pelee Island occupation.

Image of Benjamin Wait, from the cover of his memoirs.

In June 1838, Wait joined the Short Hills raid in the Niagara area. The British captured most of the invaders and later transported Wait and others to Van Diemen's Land.

In his book on the Patriot War, Robert B. Ross includes an account of the Pelee Island battle allegedly given by "Major" Wait fifty years later. It is mostly fiction. In it, Wait said he became commander after Colonel Seward stepped down. He paints himself as a hero who, through military cunning and firm control of the men, defeats the British and inflicts heavy casualties. Wait wrote that the Patriots charged the British line with bayonets, scattering them. Outnumbered, Wait said they abandoned the island as clear victors. No accounts of the Pelee Island occupation except Wait's describe him playing any role in the final battle.

HENRY VAN RENSSELAER

Henry H. Van Rensselaer (1806–1838) was the son of Major General Henry K. Van Rensselaer and a first cousin of the Patriot commander General Rensselaer Van Rensselaer. Like his older cousin, Henry was a scion of an established, wealthy and respected New York clan. Unlike his timid cousin, Henry was fearless. In the Battle of Pelee Island, Henry stood at the front ranks of his men, keeping order and discipline until mortally wounded. The first deaths the British military suffered in the Patriot War came during this battle. Much of the claim or blame falls on Henry.

On March 12, 1838, General McLeod sent Henry's mother a letter of condolence, which read in part:

> *DEAR MADAM:*
> *I have just arrived in town, and it is with great pain that I announce to you the death of your brave and heroic son, Henry Van Rensselaer, at the battle of Point au Pelee Island. He died cheering on his men to victory.*
>
> *When Canada becomes free, I assure you, a monument shall be erected to your brave and chivalrous son.*

Henry's brother Kilian H. Van Rensselaer went to Pelee Island to claim the body.

The defeat at Pelee Island ended sanctioned Patriot military campaigns in the west for nine months, but the loss of yet another battle did nothing to dampen rebel enthusiasm and optimism. The Patriot War was far from over.

Chapter 7

Sutherland and Theller Face the Courts: March and April 1838

On January 12, 1838, the Upper Canada government passed the Act to Protect the Inhabitants of This Province Against Lawless Aggressions from the Subjects of Foreign Countries at Peace with Her Majesty. Known by its abbreviated name, the Lawless Aggressions Act, the colony created it as a tool to defend itself against Patriot raids—in much the same way that modern countries passed anti-terrorism laws after September 11, 2001.

An absolute abomination, the act permitted flimsy evidence from the prosecution and few avenues of defense for the accused. It applied to attacks by citizens of a country with which Great Britain was at peace and to British subjects who aided them. The act did not require the government to disclose what evidence it had against the accused, and it prevented a defendant's lawyer from actively participating in the court-martial; they could only advise prior to trial.

The Upper Canada government used this act instead of the Treason Act. As ominous as a treason charge sounds, a treason conviction required two independent prosecution witnesses. The Treason Act respected the defendant's right to legal representation and permitted defense counsel to examine the prosecution's evidence in advance. In short, the accused received a fair trial for the standards of the time. Hardcore Upper Canada Tories were not interested in acquittals. The Treason Act also did not apply to foreigners.

The Lawless Aggressions Act became a tool to fast-track prisoners from their cells to the gallows. In any prosecution under the act, the crown needed to establish three facts: 1) the prisoner's citizenship; 2) for an American, that he conspired with British subjects, or for a British subject, that he conspired with foreign citizens; and 3) that the prisoner actively bore arms on British soil against loyal subjects of Her Majesty Queen Victoria.

Sutherland Arrested

Sutherland's sword, taken from him by Colonel Prince, is on display at the Fort Malden Museum in Amherstburg.

On February 5, 1838, Thomas Jefferson Sutherland resigned his Patriot army commission. But that did not stop him from talking, as he addressed at least one Patriot meeting just before the Battle of Fighting Island. He had no involvement in the Pelee Island raid (though some sources incorrectly state he did). He left Detroit in early March for Sandusky, Ohio, on business.

On March 4, he began a sleigh journey across frozen Lake Erie with his aide, Silvanus Spencer. Being just one day after the Pelee Island battle, Canadian and British forces were naturally on guard. Sutherland had the great misfortune to be spotted by Colonel John Prince at the mouth of the Detroit River. Colonel Prince, traveling in three sleighs with a large armed party, arrested Sutherland and locked him up at Fort Malden.

Lieutenant Colonel John Maitland wrote to his superior, "Somehow or other, I think Sutherland must have been making his way to the island [Pelee] when he was taken, but he pretends to know nothing of the action that took place." He then shipped Sutherland to Toronto for trial.

Court-martial of Sutherland

Sutherland had the dubious honor of being the first captured rebel tried under the Lawless Aggressions Act. On March 13, just nine days after his capture, he faced eight militia officers serving as the jury, Colonel James Fitzgibbon as the prosecutor and George Jarvis as judge advocate. Colonel Fitzgibbon had helped defeat William Lyon Mackenzie in Toronto. Jarvis was a judge, a conservative member of the assembly and a militia officer. Of the eight jurymen, seven held comfortable Family Compact appointments or public offices. Sutherland faced a very biased court as he defended himself.

From the moment of his capture and throughout his trial, Sutherland claimed his arrest was illegal because he was in U.S. territory. He reasoned that if his arrest was illegal, then so was his court-martial. When arrested with his aide, Sutherland's only weapon was a sword. He protested that no evidence showed that sword was used against British subjects. Sutherland correctly argued that one of the men on the jury, being a British army officer, was not "competent to sit on this court-martial" because the act required the jury to be exclusively from the militia. He stated truthfully that he had no involvement with the Pelee Island raid. He admitted to participating in the occupation of Navy Island and attack on Fort Malden, but as he argued, those events occurred before the Lawless Aggressions Act existed, and the act could not be applied to him retroactively.

Sutherland called no defense witnesses but enthusiastically cross-examined Colonel Prince and other Crown witnesses. With adjournments to allow Sutherland to prepare his defense, the trial continued until March 29. He waited in jail for one month before learning the verdict: guilty, death by hanging.

In March 1838, Sir George Arthur, former lieutenant governor of Van Diemen's Land and its penal colony, replaced Francis Bond Head as the lieutenant governor of Upper Canada just as Sutherland's trial neared its end. While always ready to hang a rebel, Arthur believed in due process. He twice voiced concerns about the case to Upper Canada's attorney general, Christopher Hagerman. Hagerman supported the conviction and explained that courts-martial were not bound to the same degree of procedural strictness as the regular courts.

Still not satisfied, Arthur asked for advice from Lord Glenelg. He found the case to be defective due to the vagueness of the original indictment, the lack of proof that

Portrait of Sir George Arthur.

Sutherland fell within the provisions of the act and various procedural anomalies, such as the composition of the jury.

Due to the admitted irregularities, the government quickly commuted Sutherland's sentence to transport for life at an unnamed penal colony. While Sutherland waited to be transferred to the Citadel prison in Quebec to await a transport ship, he became despondent over his conviction and attempted suicide by slitting veins in his arms and feet. He failed.

In the Citadel, Sutherland wrote long letters to many dignitaries, including President Martin Van Buren and Queen Victoria, arguing his case. He maintained, with evidence, that his arrest was illegal. The immediate effect of his arguments was to postpone his one-way trip to an antipodal penal colony.

There is evidence that Colonel Price arrested Sutherland in America. Sutherland and his aide were travelling in a sleigh. Another traveler on the ice, David Thompson, passed them in his sleigh that day. He swore in a deposition dated June 22, 1838, that from his vantage point, Sutherland's sleigh never strayed into Upper Canada.

TRIAL OF THELLER

Dr. Edward Alexander Theller was a colorful Patriot rebel of Irish extraction. He commanded the rebel ship captured during the first western raid in January.

Dr. Theller faced off against Upper Canada's chief justice, John Beverley Robinson, in April 1838, with the ambitious Henry Sherwood as prosecutor. Learning a lesson from the Sutherland court-martial, the Crown did not charge Dr. Theller under the Lawless Aggressions Act, since his crime occurred before the act's assent. Instead, the prosecution charged him with treason because the Crown insisted he was still a British subject.

The Crown produced several credible witnesses, and Dr. Theller never denied his involvement in the attack on Fort Malden. Conducting his own defense, Dr. Theller made three arguments: 1) that treason could not apply to him because he was no longer a British subject but a naturalized American; 2) that if he did, in fact, break any laws, it was "against the laws of nations," and he should thus be tried in a higher court in England, not a provincial court; and 3) that as an American who broke the neutrality law of the United States, he should be returned to that jurisdiction.

His first argument swayed the jury, which returned a qualified verdict: "If the prisoner is a British subject, he is guilty of treason." Citizenship rules were vague in the nineteenth century, but Dr. Theller's eleven years in the United States made him a de facto naturalized citizen by the norms of the time. The jury's verdict amounted to an acquittal but left the final decision to the court.

Chief Justice Robinson dismissed Dr. Theller's defense, stating that the obligation of natural allegiance was perpetual and inalienable. He found Dr. Theller guilty and on April 10 sentenced him to hang on April 24.

Two of Mackenzie's officers, Samuel Lount and Peter Matthews, became the first of twenty Patriot prisoners to hang in the Patriot War. From his Toronto cell, Dr. Theller watched workmen erect a scaffold in the jail's perimeter. On April 12, 1838, he witnessed both men dangle on the end of a noose. The effect chilled him and other Patriot prisoners.

Dr. Theller petitioned Lieutenant Governor Arthur to review the facts in his case. Dr. Theller stated in his memoirs that on April 23, he received a letter from George Arthur saying he saw no reason to interfere with the sentence. Dr. Theller wrote his final letters to his family and prepared for his death at dawn.

Apparently, Chief Justice Robinson had a last-minute change of heart and doubted his position on perpetual allegiance. He commuted Dr. Theller's sentence to life in an Australian penal colony. Dr. Theller's jailors told him the news just hours before the scheduled execution.

In late May, the British sent Generals Theller and Sutherland plus other Patriot prisoners to the Citadel, Quebec City's fort and military prison. Imprisoned in Quebec City with General Theller were eight survivors of his crew on the *Anne*: Theron R. Culver, Henry Hull, Abraham W. Partridge, Benjamin Pew, Chauncey Parker, Squire Thayer, Nathaniel Smith and Colonel William Wallin Dodge, who had survived his devastating eye wound. Two other former crew members of the *Anne*, Colonel Stephen Brophy and Major Walter Chase, were being held in Fort Henry at Kingston. The other seven surviving crewmen had been pardoned and deported earlier.

General Theller, being a man of action, began plotting his way out.

RELEASE OF UPPER CANADA PRISONERS

When solicitor general of Upper Canada William Draper arrived in Hamilton in March 1838 to examine evidence against men arrested in the days after Dr. Duncombe's failed uprising, he found little to substantiate the charges for twenty-four and had them released. Only twenty-seven went to trial, and only ten were convicted.

In April, Draper had a similar experience in London, where only fifteen rebels were tried and nine convicted. Even before his arrival, the courts had ordered men released.

Elias Moore posted bail on February 19, 1838, and never faced prison or trial. Likewise, Robert Always left prison March 28. Both men kept their seats in the assembly.

By August 1838, the courts had processed all men captured as suspects or participants in Dr. Duncombe's uprising. While nineteen prisoners had verdicts of treason found against them, Draper reported to his superiors that none had compounded their act of treason with murder, robbery or arson. Since no actual pitched battle had occurred, no casualties existed among loyal subjects. That fact permitted colonial officials to show mercy. And they did. No one died on the gallows for that rebellion alone.

Some participants in Duncombe's uprising who remained hardcore rebels later hanged or died during additional acts of insurrection.

Chapter 8

Lodges and Secret Societies Form: May–September 1838

B ehind the battle lines in the spring and summer of 1838, Canadian rebels and their American supporters continued to organize and raise money. It became clear to the three principal rebel organizations—the Patriot Army of the Northwest, commanded by General Henry S. Handy; the Patriots under their new commander, General Donald McLeod (General Van Rensselaer being ousted for incompetence); and *Les Patriotes*, under command of General Robert Nelson (based in Vermont and challenging Lower Canada)—that public recruitment and training made it too easy for spies and traitors to infiltrate and spoil their plans. Each army fostered a network of "secret" lodges.

General Nelson set up the *Frères-Chasseurs* to plan for another invasion of Lower Canada.

In March 1838, General McLeod joined Dr. Charles Duncombe and other Canadian Patriot leaders in Lockport, New York. They formed the Canadian Refugee Relief Association (CRRA). On the surface, it mimicked a philanthropic organization designed to help displaced Canadians. But in reality, its mission was to raise funds for continued warfare against Britain's colonies. Dr. Alexander Mackenzie, a rebel refugee from Hamilton, Upper Canada, became the first CRRA president. General McLeod took on an unofficial role as military operative and organizer of satellite committees. William Lyon Mackenzie, though a CRRA executive committee member, did not attend the inaugural meeting and played a minor and diminishing role. Mackenzie had begun to disavow violence as a means to achieve reform.

SONS OF LIBERTY

In June 1838, General Handy began building a new organization in Michigan for the liberation of Canada, called the Sons of Liberty. (Other groups in America have carried this moniker before and after General Handy's group.)

General Handy appointed special agents to journey through border states and Upper Canada to form secret lodges and recruit men who could be relied upon to aid the cause. Each agent had a pile of blank commissions signed by General Handy or one of his top generals.

In densely populated areas, General Handy's agents would appoint one man in every square mile to be captain of a lodge. In rural areas, the ratio was one captain for every ten square miles. Each captain recruited members. Lodges then elected colonels to command larger districts. By the end of June 1838, the Sons of Liberty had formed into two hundred companies of one

Copy of a blank commission in General Handy's Patriot army, signed by General E.J. Roberts, similar to those used for Sons of Liberty. The image on the left shows the American eagle carrying away the British lion. *Courtesy Fort Malden Museum.*

hundred men each (or so they said) totaling twenty thousand recruits. Each member took an oath similar to the following:

> *You do solemnly swear, in the presence of Almighty God, that you will bear allegiance and fidelity to the Sons of Liberty engaged in the Patriot service and in the cause of Canadian Independence—that you will obey the orders of your superior officers in whatever department you may serve—that you will never communicate, or in any way divulge the existence or plans of said association. You also swear that you will devote your time, your person, your interest in promoting said cause, so far as may be consistent with your other duties—that you will never sell, barter, or in any way alter any badge that may be bestowed upon you for the purpose of designating your rank in said association. You also swear that you will not disclose or in any way communicate to any person the contents or purport of this Oath and that you will not converse with any person in reference to this Oath or with the man who first presents it to you.*

General Handy used a network of one hundred couriers to communicate with the lodges. Each courier had a specific beat of ten miles to be covered daily. This way, information could be relayed immediately from General Handy to his colonels, and the regions in turn could inform their supreme commander.

One big challenge for General Handy was equipping twenty thousand men for war. He hoped to obtain weapons by the proven method of "liberating" them from the Michigan state arsenal. Among the sentinels at arsenals and jails were those who had been under his command in earlier raids or who supported the Patriot cause. By arrangement, someone at the arsenal left the windows unfastened. Miraculously, keys to the magazine at Detroit found their way into the hands of General Elijah Roberts. Between the two sites, fifteen thousand muskets or rifles, fifteen cannon and ammunition were waiting to be taken.

General Handy's plan was to raid the arsenal and magazine early on July 4, 1838. Thirty men stood ready to remove the weapons to two barges moored near the arsenal. Thus provisioned, the general next intended to mobilize the Sons of Liberty, arm them and attack Upper Canada with an overwhelming force.

In New York, General McLeod and Dr. Charles Duncombe also planned a July 4 invasion across the Niagara River.

ST. CLAIR RIVER RAIDS

History shows that General Handy had a knack for detailed invasion plans. If Thomas Jefferson Sutherland had not interfered in January 1838, General Handy's army might have easily overwhelmed the small militia contingent in the Western District at that time.

General Handy's plans for a second invasion on July 4 included a big enough army to quite possibly rout the Canadian defenders, even though their numbers had swelled with hundreds of British regulars.

History also shows that General Handy continued to have his plans foiled by lesser men. In the week leading up to July 4, word leaked out about his invasion, and several bands of freelance rebels jumped the gun with unsanctioned forays into Canada.

On June 25, a Western District settler swore before a justice of the peace that another man tried to have him join a Patriot invasion scheduled for July 4. He said rebels would attack in fifteen locations. He wasn't taken seriously until two days later.

On June 26, a gang of raiders set sail from Palmer, Michigan, in a sloop with Colonel John Vreeland in command. They crossed Lake Huron and landed at the village of Goderich, where they robbed stores and escaped. American authorities arrested several of the gang, including Colonel Vreeland. The colonel eventually had his day in court before Judge Wilkins. Colonel Vreeland became the first Patriot officer not to be acquitted by the Patriot-friendly judge.

On June 27, a band of Patriots numbering about one hundred crossed St. Clair River to Nugent's Inn (near present-day Port Lambton, Ontario). They hoisted the Patriot flag and awaited further orders, which did not come. The local militia marched to the scene and arrested six men, including innkeeper Nugent, while the others fled.

That same day, nine raiders were confronted by a group of loyalists in Dawn Township (near president-day Dresden, Ontario). Four invaded a house, and a fight broke out. One of the defenders, Captain William Kerry, died from a gunshot. The culprit blamed was William Putnam, the once pacifistic resident of London.

On June 28, 1838, a sloop belonging to Charles Bowerman landed an armed party at the Canadian village of Sombra on the St. Clair River. They robbed the town store and plundered the local commissariat, took two hostages and returned to the ship. They sailed upstream. Seventeen local militiamen and seven Chippewa warriors (part of a group of twenty-four who turned out to defend against the raiders) chased them in three log canoes. The patriots landed on the Michigan side of the river and fled. American authorities freed the hostages, returned the stolen goods and impounded the sloop.

A general panic ensued in the Western District. Lieutenant Colonel John Maitland asked for and received two additional companies of regulars. In Michigan, General Hugh Brady heard about the commotion. His suspicions alerted, he placed trusted guards on the arsenal and magazine. Deprived of weapons on the eve of the Fourth of July attack, General Handy called it off.

The incursions along the St. Clair River and the unsanctioned Short Hills assault near Niagara in June spoiled any chance of a July 4 surprise attack being executed.

During the St. Clair River raids, Canadian authorities arrested eleven men. Eight were released after their trials in late September. The exceptions were Horace Cooley, William Herrington and Charles Bowerman. Bowerman and Cooley were convicted of burglary and condemned to hang. Early in 1839, the courts released Herrington and Bowerman on bail. Cooley, who had also been caught the previous winter carrying Patriot dispatches between Upper Canada and Michigan (Cooley may have been one of General Handy's couriers), received little mercy. In September 1839, Cooley boarded the *Buffalo* with scores of other Patriot convicts bound for the penal colony in Van Diemen's Land. He never came home.

HUNTERS LODGE

In May 1838, Patriot leaders, including General McLeod, laid the foundation of a new organization that would soon eclipse every other existing secret society founded on the goal of liberating Canada.

Called the Hunters Lodge, or Patriot Hunters, the first grand lodge appeared in St. Albans, Vermont. Other grand lodges followed in Cleveland, Ohio (the western headquarters); Rochester, New York (the eastern headquarters); Buffalo, New York; Detroit, Michigan; and Montreal, Lower Canada.

Hunters held four degrees of membership: snowshoe, beaver, master hunter and patriot hunter. Members were initiated as snowshoes and learned new secret signs and passwords at each stage. Recruits recited secret oaths on their knees, blindfolded, with knives pointed at their throats. Betrayal

Multiple sources suggest that the Hunters Lodge took its name from Dr. James Hunter, a Canadian Patriot who marched with William Lyon Mackenzie. The similarity is a coincidence. The name came from Nelson's group, Frères-Chasseurs, which translates into "hunter brothers" or "hunter brotherhood."

of lodge secrets meant death. A member's house could be burned for disobeying orders.

Senior Hunter leaders tended to also be Masons—in fact, the term Patriot Masons became an occasionally used synonym for the Hunters Lodge. Freemason affiliation cemented their positions in the new brotherhood and gave them ample experience with oaths, secret rituals and related arcana. Many junior officers and even privates also claimed membership in the Masons.

While the Hunter leaders bragged that they had thousands of armed men ready to fight, few men had any interest in war. Hunter membership became the best way to make business and political connections in difficult times. The depression and ongoing banking crises gripping the U.S. border states united the diverse classes. Politicians, merchants, businessmen, mechanics, farmers and common laborers joined the lodge. Motivations varied. For many, the Hunters movement was an altruistic attempt to give Canada a republican government. Others foresaw a chance to make money. Profiteers, land speculators and carpetbaggers mixed with the honest idealists.

Fascination with the Hunters caught hold and spread through the border towns like fire in dry grass. With great fanfare, new lodges opened weekly. By the end of summer 1838, Hunters had set up hundreds of lodges in America. They ranged from Maine to Wisconsin and as far inland as Kentucky. At their height, the Hunters claimed 200,000 members, though 40,000 is probably more accurate. Hunter cells also formed in Upper and Lower Canada, but quietly.

In a few short months, the Hunters Lodge became the largest and best funded of the militaristic secret orders. With their effective fundraising apparatus and endorsement by prominent men, the Hunters stole members from Mackenzie's original Patriots, General McLeod's Canadian Refugee Relief Association and General Handy's Sons of Liberty.

HUNTERS LODGE PLANS TAKEOVER OF CANADA

By September 1838, the Hunters Lodge had achieved a significant level of political influence, claiming as members Michigan governor Stevens T. Mason and Vice President Richard Mentor Johnson. It had developed military muscle through stealing or buying weapons and by recruiting numerous militia officers into its ranks.

From September 16 to 22, influential Hunters held a convention in Cleveland, Ohio, to pick new leaders for pending invasions of Canada that fall and to create a provisional government. (Most sources estimate the number of attendees at 160.) There is no clear mention of where the Hunters held their convention in the city. They most likely gathered in the Hunters' grand lodge western headquarters in the Miller Block. It was an early, four-story commercial building in central Cleveland at number 197 on old Superior Street, amongst a row of similar office buildings between the former streets of Seneca and Bank. The Hunters rented the upper floor, which included a spacious hall used for meetings and drilling recruits. For a secret society, they never made an effort to hide their business. (The current location equates to West Superior Avenue between West Third Street and West Sixth Street. Cleveland does boast a 1905 building called the Miller Block on a different street.)

The big names at the meetings included Dr. Charles Duncombe, General Donald McLeod, Captain Gilman Appleby and Patriot Admiral Bill Johnston. Western Patriot leader General Henry S. Handy and Lower Canada's Patriot leader General Robert Nelson sent representatives. No one invited William Lyon Mackenzie, the man who started it all.

Ambitious new leaders and men with high social standing also came out in force to grab a piece of the rising star, including: Bernard Bagley, a wealthy and influential lawyer from Watertown, New York; Lucius Verus Bierce, a lawyer and brigadier general in the militia from Akron, Ohio; John Grant, the collector of customs from Oswego, New York; militia colonel Loving P. Harris, a businessman from Amherst, Ohio; Abram Daniel Smith, a physician from Cleveland, Ohio; Benjamin Stone, a wealthy grocer from Upper Canada; and Nathan Williams, a Cleveland grocer and colonel in the Ohio militia.

The conventioneers elected Smith, twenty-seven, as president of the republican government in waiting. Had the Hunters succeeded in overthrowing Upper Canada, President Smith's face might grace Canada's ten-dollar bill today instead of Prime Minister John A. Macdonald. Delegates elected Colonel Williams as vice-president.

Old Superior Street in central Cleveland near where the Miller Block stood. Taken from C.E. Bailliere's *The New World in 1859.*

Surprisingly, the delegates elected Bierce, thirty-seven, as the Hunter army's commander-in-chief. He beat out the favorite, General Handy.

According to historian Charles Lindsey, William Putnam and other western Patriots urged the delegates to select Bierce over General Handy. Lindsey wrote, "Gen. Handy seems to have been poorly repaid by his associates for all his exertions and sacrifices."

The convention affirmed Johnston, the infamous Thousand Islands smuggler and pirate, as navy commodore in the St. Lawrence River and

Lake Ontario. Captain Appleby became navy commodore on Lake Erie. General McLeod rose to secretary of war.

At the urging of Dr. Duncombe, they laid the groundwork for a financial arm, the Republican Bank of Canada. The bank's notes were to bear the faces of executed Patriots. Grant became president of the bank and Bagley a vice-president.

At the convention, Hunter leaders in the west and east agreed to launch simultaneous attacks in early November near Windsor and on the St. Lawrence River. Robert Nelson also picked November for his next assault on Lower Canada.

Spies for both nations were in good attendance and reported the events to their masters.

Despite its formation as a secret society, the Hunters continued to communicate publicly. For example, Colonel Williams and General Robert Nelson both began distributing circulars in October 1838 warning supporters to be prepared for an invasion of Canada on November 1.

LUCIUS VERUS BIERCE

Image of Lucius Verus Bierce from his days as mayor of Akron. Bierce was described as five feet, ten inches tall, with a light complexion and a tendency toward being overweight.

Lucius Verus Bierce was born in Cornwall, Connecticut, in 1801. His parents originally came from England and lived for a time in Nova Scotia. In 1817, his father settled in Nelson, Ohio, his mother being recently deceased. One week later, at age fifteen, Bierce left home and moved to the university town of Athens. He wanted a proper education, but his father couldn't afford to support his studies. So for five years, Lucius worked any job he could find to earn money for university and living costs. He graduated with a BA in 1822.

After graduation, Bierce walked—having no money for transportation—to South Carolina to study law. The next spring, he walked to Alabama to continue his studies. On September 12, 1823, the State of Alabama accepted him as a licensed attorney. A month later, he walked back to Ohio and settled in Ravenna to be near his elderly father. There, he continued his law studies. In 1824, he was admitted to the Ohio bar. In 1825, he accepted an appointment as district attorney. He held that position for eleven years, after which he moved to Akron, Ohio. In 1838, like so many Americans, he was drawn to the idealism of the Patriot War.

ABRAM DANIEL SMITH

Abram Daniel Smith was born in Lowville, New York, in 1811. He later settled in Sackets Harbor, where he studied law. He studied medicine at the Castleton Medical School in Vermont, where he graduated in 1831. He married in 1832, and the couple had their first child in 1834. In 1836, the family moved to Cleveland, Ohio, where Smith quickly rose to prominence in the community. He won a spot on city council and joined the board of a girls' school. He became a practitioner of and lecturer on phrenology. Like many politicians, he gravitated toward the new and influential Hunters Lodge, where he quickly gained influence. Once

Portrait of Abram Daniel Smith as a Wisconsin Supreme Court justice.

declared president, he set up his war office in the Hunters' grand lodge in the old Miller Block. Witness accounts state that the office building saw frequent visitors at all hours of the day.

GILMAN APPLEBY

Gilman Appleby was born in Bethlehem, New Hampshire, on August 29, 1806. As adults, he and his younger brother Calvin became sailors on Lakes Erie, Huron and Michigan. Both began their careers as hands on small vessels and earned their way up the ranks to captain. Gilman married in November 1825.

Gilman was skipper of the *Caroline* on the night Captain Andrew Drew and his crew attacked the steamer and torched it. Gilman, slightly wounded by a sword, jumped overboard and hid under the wharf. If Gilman was not a rebel supporter before then, he was after the incident.

When the Hunters appointed him navy commodore on Lake Erie, the lodge had no formal navy but did brag that it controlled several steamers. For example, Appleby owned the steamer *Constitution*.

Nils von Schoultz

Finnish-born Nils Sholtewskii von Schoultz (1807–1838) came to America in 1836 and established himself as a successful salt manufacturer in Salina, New York. Von Schoultz always claimed to have served as an officer in a Swedish artillery regiment, fought the Russians in Poland with Polish freedom fighters and served with the French Foreign Legion in Africa.

Intrigued by how closely the conversations on Canadian liberation matched his experiences in Poland, von Schoultz joined the Hunters and communicated his eagerness to serve the cause. Von Schoultz claimed to have five hundred Polish exiles in Philadelphia ready to fight. General Bierce sent him a letter dated September 17, 1838, inquiring about the organization and readiness of his troops. In his September 28, 1838 reply to the general, von Schoultz laid out an elaborate campaign to invade Upper Canada. First, he would take a regiment by water and occupy Fort Erie, Upper Canada. From there, they would march to Queenston and take over the town and its fortifications. Leaving behind a small garrison, he planned to march to Fort George on the Niagara River and take it and the nearby village.

On the same day he attacked Fort George, the plan called for General Bierce to cross the Detroit River and capture the now rebuilt and heavily manned Fort Malden. Then, after leaving a garrison to hold the fort, Bierce was supposed to march straight across southern Ontario, through London, to Ancaster, near Hamilton. Once there, General Bierce was to alert von Schoultz at Fort George of the approximate date that General Bierce would be in place to attack Toronto. Von Schoultz would then sail his army to attack that city from the lake at the same hour.

What von Schoultz proposed to accomplish in mere days with a few regiments of untrained civilians is exactly what the U.S. armed forces had failed to achieve in the three years of the War of 1812. Von Schoultz clearly had no knowledge of the geographical span of the colony or the size and capacity of the colonial defense forces.

General Bierce seems to have bought into von Schoultz's wildly ambitious and unworkable plan. In his memoirs, Bierce indicates that he made preparatory plans for the invasion. He wrote that he ordered von Schoultz and his regiment of Poles to Detroit and ordered General John Ward Birge, a commander of a Hunter army in New York, to move his men to Buffalo to "hold themselves in readiness to cross and fortify Fort Erie."

Some weeks later, General Bierce learned that General Birge had ignored his order and planned his own invasion near Prescott in eastern Upper Canada. Bierce immediately sent a message to General Birge to "stop the wild scheme," which General Birge refused to do.

Bierce claimed that he hurried in person to prevent the attack. When he arrived in Buffalo, he learned he was too late. He could not prevent the disastrous invasion that became known as the Battle of the Windmill. (That event is described in detail in a companion book published by The History Press, *The Patriot War Along the New York-Canada Border*.)

Chapter 9

Theller and Dodge Escape: October 1838

While being held in the Toronto jail, Dr. Edward Theller shared cells with three rebels convicted for their part in Mackenzie's rebellion: John Montgomery, Gilbert Morden and John Anderson. In May, the British moved those four and twenty other prisoners to other prisons. Dr. Theller and about half the prisoners filled cells at the Quebec City Citadel, while his three former cellmates and others took up lodging at Fort Henry in Kingston.

Montgomery, Morden, Anderson and nine others successfully escaped from Fort Henry on July 29, 1838, on a stormy night. Montgomery severely injured his leg during his escape. Two prisoners who helped him hobble to freedom were men captured with Dr. Theller on the *Anne*: Stephen Brophy and Walter Chase.

News of their breakout from the impregnable fort inspired Dr. Theller and those of his *Anne* crew incarcerated with him in the equally hard-to-escape-from Citadel. They began discussing how to break out of their prison. Dr. Theller managed, through legitimate visitors to the Citadel, to pass letters to friends on the outside asking for help. Those friends in return gave Dr. Theller details about the configuration of outer walls and ditches and the position of sentinels. One man slipped Dr. Theller escape tools during a visit.

One of Dr. Theller's outside friends was Charles Drolet, forty-five, a lawyer, an elected member of the Lower Canada assembly and a member of the secretive rebel group *Frères-Chasseurs*. He conferred with Dr. Theller on the ramparts of the Citadel in plain sight of guards.

Engraving of an 1840 print by William Henry Bartlett showing the view from the Quebec City Citadel.

Dr. Theller's men began sawing through an iron bar in their cell window. One man would saw while others created distractions: one played the fife, others noisily carved toys from wood and one, usually Dr. Theller, conversed with the guard.

The bar took many days to cut through. When each day's work ended, they filled the incision with tallow darkened with soot. With the bar finally cut and barely held in place, Dr. Theller's gang waited for an evening of inclement weather, just as Montgomery had back in July. When the night came, each man in the escape group put on extra clothing and rolled up belongings in their cloaks.

Dr. Theller had purposely made friends with many of the guards through long conversations through the bars of the cell door. On October 23, 1838, the night before the British intended to put Dr. Theller on a ship for England, he persuaded his guard to share a farewell drink with him. Dr. Theller had managed to obtain a supply of porter and rum and a quantity of laudanum. His guard requested porter. Dr. Theller obliged after first secretly adding the liquid opiate to the drinking vessel.

Soon, the guard was so inebriated that he leaned against the bars of the cell for support. Even then, Dr. Theller had to hold him up to prevent him slumping to the floor.

The jailbreak began. The now one-eyed rebel William Wallin Dodge went first. He tied a series of knotted sheets to a window bar and let the improvised rope down to a lower level where the escapees would gather. Men began slipping through the open window. When Dr. Theller's turn came to leave, Squire Thayer took Dr. Theller's place holding up the guard through the door's bar and bid his commander a bon voyage.

Dr. Theller found his stout figure a serious impediment. He could not slip through the gap in the window bars. By removing two layers of upper garments he pushed through with help from Partridge, receiving scrapes on his back in the process.

One by one, five men gathered outside the window: Dodge, Chauncey Parker, Theron Culver, Henry Hull and Dr. Theller. Abraham W. Partridge, Benjamin Pew, Squire Thayer and Nathaniel Smith stayed behind.

When the last man came down, a cellmate that had remained behind pulled the sheets back into the cell.

The would-be escapees crouched in silence as the guards changed shifts. They crossed the parade ground on their bellies past several sentries, relying on the dark as cover.

Parker, in a fear-induced delirium, strayed as he crossed the yard. Spotted by guards, his presence alerted all the sentinels. Guards checked Parker's cell and discovered the absence of the other four. A general alert swept the Citadel.

At that point, Dr. Theller and friends stood on the top of the outer wall. They cut the halyard from a flagpole, intending to use the rope to descend to the ground. Dodge suggested that the noise from the rope's pulley would give them away. Dr. Theller agreed and decided they all must jump the fifteen feet to the ground, and he volunteered to go first. He surmised that if he, the heaviest of them, could survive, then they all could. He hung from the wall by his hands and then let go. He dropped feet first onto solid rock and fell backward, hitting his head. Injured but conscious and mobile, he ordered the others to wait. Before anyone else jumped, he had them toss down all their coats and cloaks. These he piled to form a softer landing spot.

Culver came next; he missed the pile of clothes and fractured his leg. Hull and Dodge followed, both landing on the pile unhurt. Dodge brought several yards of the halyard with him, which they used to descend other spots at the base of the wall and into the fort's dry ditch.

After climbing out of the ditch using gaps in the stone wall as footholds, they made their way to the shore of the St. Lawrence as guards with torches searched for them. Dr. Theller limped badly. Culver couldn't walk without support from Dodge and Hull.

Hull and Culver hid behind a garden wall in the town surrounding the Citadel, while Dodge and Dr. Theller set out to get assistance from the doctor's friends. Hours later, they found sanctuary in the home of a Patriot sympathizer. Dodge departed with two supporters to get Hull and Culver. By that point, soldiers and police were combing the streets of Quebec City for the escapees, making the rendezvous impossible. Cold and feeling abandoned, Hull and Culver entered a tavern for warmth. The proprietor sent a servant to inform the Citadel guards. Both men returned to the prison in irons.

Sympathizers hustled Dodge and Dr. Theller in disguise separately out of town. They reunited at a farm days later. With help from Patriot sympathizers, including Drolet, they made their way across country to the Maine border in early November. Welcomed and feted as a hero in the United States, Dr. Theller toured border towns preaching the righteous Patriot cause and regularly denouncing Sutherland as a coward and fink.

A copy of the advertising circular for the Patriot meeting featuring Dr. Theller and Mackenzie in Washington, D.C. *Library of Congress.*

On November 28, 1838, Dr. Theller took his message to the American capital, where he and William Lyon Mackenzie spoke to Patriot and Hunter sympathizers in Washington. At the suggestion of the mayor, they agreed to address supporters of the cause in Carusi's Saloon, an establishment big enough to hold a large crowd. The publicly advertised meeting drew condemnation from officials connected to President Martin Van Buren, who put pressure on government employees to stay away. Despite that, 1,500 people attended, and hundreds joined the lodge, where "full four-fifths of them were clerks and officers connected with some of the departments of the government," wrote Dr. Theller.

Dr. Theller united with his family in Detroit on December 4, 1838. Two days later, American authorities arrested and charged him with violations of the U.S. neutrality laws but released him on bail pending trial. After a four-day trial in June 1839, the jury acquitted him after ten minutes of deliberation. With his acquittal, the prosecutor dropped similar charges against Dodge and Brophy.

In his 1841 memoirs, Dr. Theller took credit for the escape plan and wrote that he and his eight companions had to keep cellmate Thomas Jefferson Sutherland ignorant of their plans during the escape preparations. Dr. Theller claimed Sutherland spied on them to win favor for his release and that his group despised Sutherland and made no effort to hide it. Dr. Theller's account of Sutherland is one of many examples in his book in which he drifts into mendacity.

In a letter to publisher Horace Greeley printed in the August 30, 1844 *New York Daily Tribune*, Sutherland denounced any suggestion that he betrayed Dr. Theller at the Citadel. Under Sutherland's letter, the newspaper ran a letter dated May 10, 1839, signed by five of Dr. Theller's cellmates— Culver, Hull, Partridge, Thayer and Smith—refuting Dr. Theller. They said Sutherland drew up the escape plan but did not participate because he had been informed that he would soon be released on bail. Further, wrote the five, the warden punished Sutherland for the escapes by putting him in the "black hole" for five weeks and removing privileges.

Dr. Theller's return to in Detroit on December 4, 1838, gave him a front-row seat for the last major invasion of the Patriot War.

Chapter 10

Windsor Invaded: December 1838

The top generals of the Hunter and Patriot armies promised at the Cleveland convention in September 1838 to invade the Canadian colonies in early November. They expected that simultaneous raids would weaken and divide the British and Canadian defenders.

Dr. Robert Nelson kept his part of the bargain. On November 3, 1838, about the same day that Dr. Edward Theller slipped into Maine, secret cells of insurgents rose up in various towns south of Montreal, while an army of three thousand fighters mobilized in Vermont. Short on weapons, General Nelson's troops put up a good fight, even winning a few small battles. Still, five thousand British regulars and thousands of Lower Canada militiamen crushed the last uprising of Les Patriotes in one week.

In New York State, Hunter general John Ward Birge pulled together a well-armed force of several thousand men. The eager Nils von Schoultz deserted General Bierce and pledged his services and his Polish troops to General Birge. Through a series of blunders and delays and Birge's dubious leadership, a mere 182 Hunters invaded Canada near Prescott, across the river from Ogdensburg, New York, on November 12, 1838. They took over a hamlet of stone houses and a stone windmill. They held off a superior British force for four days before surrendering.

As leader of the disastrous Battle of the Windmill, von Schoultz learned the hard way about the true strength and tenacity of the Canadian defenders and the inherent weaknesses of the Hunter Lodge organization. Only three or four Polish exiles joined von Schoultz in his suicidal folly. (The Battle of the Windmill is detailed in *The Patriot War Along the New York-Canada Border*.)

BIERCE LATE TO THE GAME

The man elected as top general of the Hunter army, Lucius Verus Bierce, failed to deliver an invasion on the western front in November. For several reasons, military action from Michigan and Ohio was slow in coming, even though General Bierce had an army of eager Patriots and Hunters mobilized near Detroit and Sandusky.

One hitch may have been yet another weapons shortage. On November 24, General Hugh Brady captured a ship carrying thirteen cases of rifles (about 250) bound for General Bierce. With General Brady's men watching every rebel move, another challenge was obtaining a ship to cross the river.

Well before the raid, General Brady had told the British about the gatherings of suspected rebels in Michigan. Canadian observers and spies tracked every move of General Bierce's army from early November to December 2, 1838. Estimates put the potential invaders at between four hundred and six hundred. Those were anxious weeks for residents along the Canadian shore.

In defense of the colony, Colonel John Prince had about two hundred militia at the ready near Windsor. Hundreds of British regulars, artillery and militia were stationed at Fort Malden.

Everyone foresaw a pending assault. By December 3 though, Canadians began to relax because they thought General Brady's confiscation of arms and the icy conditions of the river made an attack impossible.

REBEL OFFICERS FORCE BIERCE'S HAND

With the onset of wintry weather in late November, some of General Bierce's recruits abandoned the chilly camps for home. Seeing the army seep away, senior officers, including Generals Elijah Jackson Roberts and William Putnam, urged immediate action. (Reports of Putnam's rank vary, with some referring to him as colonel and others as brigadier general. The more reliable sources—Lindsey and McLeod—use the latter.) Another man urging immediate action was Brigadier General Salathiel S. Coffinberry, a newspaperman from Ohio. He'd brought a regiment of volunteers from Ohio and Pennsylvania to Detroit and wanted them to see action.

Because of their limited weaponry and dwindling numbers of men, General Bierce hesitated to press on with the attack. According to Dr.

Edward Theller, when General Bierce mentioned his misgivings to the meeting of officers, he was met with catcalls of "coward" and "traitor." Generals Putnam and Roberts and Colonel Harvell (first name unknown) offered to lead the men if General Bierce would not.

He denied their charges and said he would lead them to Canada immediately just to prove them wrong. With that, the rebels tread quietly through Detroit to the harbor and commandeered the steamboat *Champlain* at its moorings close to midnight on December 3. They forced its captain and crew to get the steam up and cross the river.

Marching with General Bierce that day were several junior officers, fugitives from Dr. Duncombe's uprising a year earlier, including Joshua Doan, Cornelius Cunningham and Daniel Bedford. Among the ranks were men who would later add their accounts of the battle and its aftermath to the historical record: Elijah Woodman, Samuel Snow, Jedediah Hunt and Robert Marsh.

John H. Harmon, twenty, also accompanied General Bierce that day as his aide-de-camp, even though the general had urged Harmon not to abandon the safety of Detroit.

Samuel Snow

Samuel D. Snow, one of the invaders that day, was born in Massachusetts in 1800 or 1801. By the start of the Patriot War, he was a miller, married with four children and living in Strongsville, Ohio (southwest of Cleveland).

Snow's rebel inspiration came while listening to an inflammatory lecture given by Dr. Duncombe in Cleveland about the lack of Canadian liberty. While Snow's memoirs put the date of that lecture at 1836 or 1837, his dates are off. Dr. Duncombe was not preaching rebellion that early. He did lecture on the Patriot cause in Cleveland in March 1838.

Snow left his comfortable life in November 1838 and journeyed to Detroit to enlist under General William Putnam.

During the Patriot War, tens of thousands of Americans pledged money and materials to help the Canadian rebels win political freedom in Upper Canada. A smaller number—between one thousand and two thousand—actually took up arms and risked their lives by invading Canada. Most of these were the so-called ordinary man—farmers, laborers and tradesmen. Samuel Snow was one of these—the only difference being that he wrote about it.

Jedediah Hunt

Jedediah Hunt Jr. was born in Candor, New York, in 1815. His involvement in the Patriot War may have stemmed partly from unfinished business: his father, Jedediah Sr. (1782–1864), had served as a captain in the New York volunteers during the War of 1812 and had fought in the Battle of Lundy's Lane.

James Dougall

One of the Windsor citizens who voluntarily joined the fray as a defender was local businessman James Dougall. Born in Scotland in 1810, he came to Canada as a young man with his father and brother.

Dougall opened the first general store in Sandwich, Upper Canada, in about 1830. He married Susanne Baby in 1832, and the couple had five sons and two daughters. That marriage connected him to the influential Baby family headed by brothers Jacques and Francois Baby (more often referred to by their Anglicized names, James and Francis). In 1834, Dougall became an agent for the Commercial Bank.

General Handy's earlier preparations for invasion in January 1838 rattled the residents of the Windsor-Sandwich area. They had a small, under-equipped and under-funded militia. Dougall loaned $12,000 to the militia to buy weapons and food and sold them $14,000 worth of clothing and blankets at cost.

Battle Begins

In the predawn darkness of December 4, the small army of Hunter and Patriot officers and men sailed the short gap across the Detroit River on the commandeered steamer and landed near the village of Walkerville, north of colonial Windsor. The number of fighters varies with the source but is most commonly estimated between 137 and 164. Bierce later stated that he had the lesser number in his force. Based on the statistics of invaders killed or captured, his number seems the most likely.

General Bierce's raiders marched south. At approximately 4:00 a.m., they entered Windsor, then a village of about three hundred. They immediately

An 1836 painting of Detroit as seen from Canada by W.J. Bennett based on a sketch by Fred Crain. *Library of Congress.*

attacked the barracks, a small wood-frame building occupied by a local militia company. The fact that the attackers got almost to Windsor without being spotted indicates a lack of vigilance.

William Baby later related that the militia captain stationed in Windsor did a poor job:

> *His sentinels were placed without judgment, and their duties were performed in the most slovenly and unsoldier-like manner. Indeed, it became too apparent to every reflecting observer that the post was liable and likely to be surprised whenever the enemy might think proper to make the experiment.*

Baby wrote that three loyalists in Detroit returned to Windsor on the afternoon of December 3 and insisted an invasion was likely that day or next. Two of those men defended the barracks when the attack began. Baby did not mention their names but claimed that "they fell martyrs to loyalty and love of country while gallantly defending the barracks."

General Bierce's original plan was to approach the barracks silently in the dark and take the defenders captive without firing a shot. According to Baby, a cavalry patrol nixed that plan:

From [the landing site], *the brigands marched down to Windsor without being challenged or opposed. When they had nearly arrived at the barracks, two of their number, who had been sent in advance to reconnoiter, were met and challenged by the cavalry patrol. As they did not answer the challenge, the patrol turned and rode back to the barracks and, relating the circumstance to the sentinel, proceeded to report to* [militia] *Capt. Lewis, whose quarters were about one-quarter of a mile further down the road.*

As soon as the two men had approached within sight of the sentinel, he challenged and, receiving no answer, leveled his piece to fire, the enemy simultaneously doing the same. By a singular coincidence, the pieces of both parties missed fire. The sentinel stepped inside the barracks to reprime and give the alarm. When he stepped out again, he found the head of a column of brigands had reached the point where he had first seen the two men. He fired his piece at this body and again entered the barracks to rouse its inmates to action.

The few men on duty promptly answered the call by rushing out and opening a galling fire upon the advancing foe; killing one of their captains...and wounding several of their men. The brave sentinel (Otterbury), forcing his way through his companions to have another shot and holding up his musket to facilitate his movements, received a ball and two buckshot in his left arm, which obliged him to retire from the conflict. As long as their ammunition held out, our men made a most gallant resistance; and when it failed, ten or twelve affected their retreat, and the rest...surrendered to the enemy.

Many historians tell variations of a sad but heroic tale of an escaped slave named William Milles. Harmon and a few men broke into Milles's house to get burning embers from the hearth to start the barracks afire. They encouraged Milles to join their army. He refused and exclaimed "God save the Queen," and they shot him dead.

With the element of surprise gone, General Bierce ordered John Harmon, his aide-de-camp, to set fire to the barracks to force the defenders out. General Bierce's men took over thirty prisoners. Reports suggest at least two defenders died in the inferno. Windsor resident James Dougall later recalled seeing five burned corpses but could not ascertain if they were friend or foe.

Robert Marsh described the forty-five-minute assault on the barracks from his perspective:

We approached within ten or twelve rods, when the sentry hailed, and without waiting an answer, fired; but without effect. His fire was returned instantly, and he fell on the spot. There was a general rush to the doors, and they were commanded to surrender as prisoners of war by General Putnam...in answer to his demand we received a volley of fire arms from the windows and doors, at which time [Patriot] *Capt Lewis fell. He was the second man from me, he was a fine man; he being the first to fall, I stepped up and rolled him over to see whether he was dead or only wounded, the ball had hit him in the head, which killed him instantly.*

We were not willing to receive such a compliment without an answer; we accordingly approached the building, and a severe action commenced—our guns, as many as possible, were protruded with theirs through the windows. We discovered after four or five rounds that they had taken the precaution to lay down in order to escape our balls, and it was a lucky move for us, for it had a tendency to cause their balls to pass over our heads; so the first few volleys on either side did but little harm; on discovering their position orders were given to withdraw from the windows a few paced and fire lower, four rounds satisfied them, some thirty or forty rushed to the doors once or twice, finally finding their situation very precarious they ceased firing. Another order was then made to surrender as prisoners of war, but they did not seem willing to comply.

The firing again commenced, when a man was seen approaching the building with a firebrand but in the confusion of firearms, did not, as he afterwards said, hear the orders not to fire the building, and it was set on fire; there was a general rush made to break through our ranks; but they soon found we knew as well how to take prisoners as to hit a mark with the rifle. In taking prisoners and securing arms, we had no time to extinguish the flames that had so far advanced.

Samuel Snow was another rebel who wrote about the Windsor raid, though in a less wordy style than that of Marsh:

We went over on a steamboat obtained the night before. Upon landing, we attacked the British barracks, carried them by storm after a short but spirited resistance, and then burnt them. In this, our first performance on British soil, we had occasion to rejoice; thirty or forty prisoners fell into our hands, and some sixty or eighty stands of arms.

Marsh stated that they took thirty-eight prisoners—a number that seems to agree with most accounts. But having no means to detain prisoners, Marsh

This 1977 painting by C.H. Forster reconstructs the Battle of Windsor. *Courtesy Fort Malden Museum.*

said the Patriots took their weapons and let them go on the promise that they would not "be found in arms against us." Whether Marsh's version is exact or not, the Patriots did not detain the prisoners for long.

By 6:00 a.m. on December 4, the invaders controlled Windsor. With the destruction of the barracks feeling like victory, General Bierce read aloud the following proclamation:

> *Soldiers! The time has arrived that calls for action—the blood of our slaughtered countrymen cries aloud for revenge. The spirits of Lount, and Matthews, and Moreau, are yet unavenged. The murdered heroes of Prescott lie in an unhallowed grave in the land of tyranny. The manes of the ill-fated* Caroline's *crew can only be appeased by the blood of the murderers. Arouse, then, soldiers of Canada! Let us avenge their wrongs! Let us march to victory or death and ever, as we meet the tyrant foe, let our war cry be: "Remember Prescott."*

The rebel force split into groups. The separation of the troops did not sit well with the men, according to Jedediah Hunt:

By this movement, the two divisions, the one under Gen. Bierce and the one under Gen. Putnam, became separated, and as a matter of consequence, served to weaken our ability for prosecuting a regular battle; and what was more, it disheartened many of our men, who, instead of making preparations for the encounter, thought only of escape.

One group of thirty to forty, including General Bierce and Harmon, was led by General Coffinberry. His company initially moved into Windsor's center to hold the village. With them were the Canadian prisoners. According to Harmon, he and three others marched to the Windsor docks and set a small streamer, the *Thames*, aflame as payback for the *Caroline*, along with two houses. The conflagration, easily seen from Detroit's waterfront, elicited cheers from thousands of onlookers who turned out to view but not participate in the battle.

The largest group of about one hundred, led by General Putnam and Colonel Cornelius Cunningham, took a position in an orchard behind the house belonging to Francois Baby on the edge of town. It was at about this point in the battle, with the barracks and steamer burning, that Marsh began to have misgivings despite the appearance of victory:

We were three hours anxiously waiting for promised help from the other side of the river, which was nearly one mile across to Detroit, where were thousands to be seen at daylight, on tops of buildings swinging their hats and cheering us on our morning's success. Among these were hundreds that had promised to be with us and who knew it was impossible for us to maintain our position through the day unless we had the promised help. If we had have known that help could not come in time, we might have re-crossed to the American shore that morning.

General Putnam's ultimate destination is unclear, but he had no opportunity to go beyond the orchard.

DEFENDERS GATHER

The Windsor militia, alerted by ringing church bells, guided by the flaming barracks and augmented by armed residents, raced to confront the main body of Hunters and Patriots in the orchard.

James Dougall was out of bed within minutes after hearing the first shots. He emptied the Commercial Bank safe to prevent it from being looted, put the money in his pockets and headed to battle. Shotgun in hand, he guided the militia to his father-in-law's orchard, where General Putnam stationed his force.

General Putnam's men were just in the process of raising the Patriot flag when the first wave of militia reinforcements came into view at about 6:30 a.m. Initially just sixty in number, the well-trained militia lined up behind a wooden-rail fence. Many Patriots assumed they had encountered professional soldiers, British regulars, because this particular militia company wore scarlet uniforms. That assumption had a chilling effect, according to Hunt:

> *I knew too well that we had no business with British regulars. Had they been only the militia and volunteers, we could have played to their hand in good earnest. A sort of panic raced through the whole Patriot force; but there was no alternative left us but to meet the emergency as best we could.*

Another sixty militiamen soon arrived. They moved unseen along a ditch and behind fences and popped up on the left flank and to the rear of General Putnam's men. Together, the militia companies attacked the Hunters from multiple directions.

According to Baby's account, General Putnam's men held their ground and returned fire until one company of militia came at them with bayonets. The survivors turned and ran for the woods.

Though his estimate of the number of militia deaths is incorrect, Hunt's account clearly captured the confusion and terror of the battle:

> *We had scarcely got in line before a volley from the regulars was poured in upon us, from a quarter we least expected it; and immediately in our rear. We wheeled and returned the compliment, but in such a confused and hurried manner that I do not suppose three balls did the slightest execution on either side. The most of us fired too high. We reloaded and poured another volley into their midst, and by this time, the firing on both sides became general. One or two attempts were made on the part of the regulars to charge upon us, but a volley from our division would check them. During this time, a number on both sides fell dead or badly wounded.*
>
> *While thus engaged, another detachment of the enemy came up and endeavored to get between us and the woods in order to cut off our retreat, and to divert our attention. A volley was fired into them, killing two. We*

instantly made the attempt to charge on them, but they fled in an opposite direction; and in looking around, we found the detachment loose upon us and in full charge.

The regularity of their movements, the uniformity of their dress, and brightness of their muskets—this mingled with the mourning groans of the wounded—struck a panic on the majority of our men, and escape seemed their only thought. About thirty actually threw down their guns and ran for the woods.

The infection soon spread among our men, and presently the whole number, with some few notable exceptions and against every persuasion and entreaty of General Putnam and Col. Harvell, joined in the retreat. Perceiving that to remain was certain death, I took up my line of march with the flying fugitives, turning now and then, as many did too, and discharging my gun, at our pursuers. The air seemed alive with screeching balls; and the most I dreaded was being wounded while flying. A bad scar to exhibit to posterity.

Samuel Snow stood with General Putnam in the orchard that day. His account seems to confirm a short battle and a rout, though he exaggerates the size of the militia:

We arrived at an orchard and halted, when we soon discovered about four hundred regulars and militia approaching us, and were soon convinced of the manner in which they intended to make our acquaintance. After the exchange of a few shots, we were ordered by our commander to retreat to a wood nearby. In this short action, and in our retreat, several of our men were killed and wounded.

The more dramatic recollections of Marsh recalled events differently, though he shares Snow's talent for enlarging the size of the enemy force:

Instantly, we were formed in battle array. Soon received a volley, but the distance was so great that it did not affect us in the least. We, however, advanced to meet them and drove them back about fifty rods. They were, I should judge, about four hundred strong, and were soon reinforced by some two hundred more. When they discovered our strength, the plan was immediately formed to surround us. A general fight now took place; but seeing their determination to surround us, after seven or eight rounds, we thought it best to occupy the woods three-fourths of a mile from our stand.

The combined volleys of musket fire from the militia devastated the invaders in the orchard. Some dropped their weapons and fled for a forest to the rear. A score of them fell either dead or wounded, Colonel Harvell among them. When he fell, the few Patriots still in the orchard retreated to the woods behind the village. A local blacksmith and newly appointed militia lieutenant named Pierre Marentette, thirty-nine, got the credit for Colonel Harvell's demise.

Just as the battle in the orchard began, Dr. John Hume, an army major, rode into the village. Alerted by the gunfire, he believed his duty as a surgeon was to attend to any wounded even though he'd been warned that raiders from Detroit controlled the streets. Witnesses state that he refused to surrender when ordered to by General Coffinberry's men. Hume turned and tried to flee to safety in a nearby house but found the door locked. He attempted to hide but was followed by several men, confronted and killed with a bayonet and musket shots. General Bierce took Hume's sword as a souvenir. (Men on both sides of the conflict later recalled Hume's killing as cowardly and unnecessary.) Hume's grave bears a strong political message:

> *Sacred to the memory of John James Hume, Esquire, MD, staff assistant surgeon who was infamously murdered and his body afterwards brutally mangled by a gang of armed ruffians from the United States styling themselves as PATRIOTS who committed this cowardly and shameful outrage on the morning of the 4th of December 1838; having intercepted the deceased while proceeding to render professional assistance to Her Majesty's gallant militia engaged at Windsor U.C. in repelling incursions of this rebel crew more properly styled PIRATES!*

General Bierce ordered Harmon to investigate the plainly audible battle in the nearby orchard. Harmon claims he rode Dr. Hume's horse—a fact disputed by Dougall, who wrote that the horse had run away—and returned with news that all was lost. Generals Bierce and Coffinberry then led a retreat to the river shore. The militia defenders did not immediately pursue General Coffinberry's company because the officers believed it to be a much larger force than in reality.

The local newspaper publisher, Henry C. Grant, joined other citizens to fight with the militia. The December 11, 1838 issue of his weekly, *The Western Herald and Farmers' Magazine*, carried a jingoistic account of the battle, short on journalistic details but long on pithy phrases such as this:

The grave of Dr. John Hume in the St. John's churchyard in Windsor. *Photo by the author.*

The straggling volunteers of Sandwich, of which we had the honor to constitute a part, came up in time to send a few leaden messengers after the fast-footed pirates, who fled with a velocity unexampled in the annals of locomotion.

Meanwhile, General Putnam rallied the retreating men and made a stand in a wooded area. Both sides exchanged gunfire. In the smoke and noise, General Putnam fell dead from a musket ball to the forehead. Hunt witnessed his death. When Putnam fell, Hunt and the others scattered. Marsh described their final defense and the vain hope that General Bierce's men would join them:

We stood our ground fighting with determined fury, until it was in vain to expect help from the rear-guard, and all hopes of holding out longer against so many, was given up, and the prospect of being surrounded and made prisoners or slaughtered on the spot, was obvious, (the latter of which I have many times since wished had been the case,) we concluded best to retreat, and commenced by walking backwards, loading and firing at intervals until we reached a fence; on getting over the fence, General Putnam was shot, with two or three others. Our ranks were then broken, some died fighting to the last, some taken prisoner, others succeeded in reaching the woods at different points, hoping to be able to rally when joined by the rear-guard and renew the attack; but failed in the attempt.

During that final shootout in the forest, the story goes that a wounded rebel raised his musket to shoot Captain Solomon Thebo of the Second Essex militia regiment. Lieutenant Pierre Marentette, observing the movement, ordered the wounded man not to fire at his company commander or he would be a dead man himself. The rebel obeyed and the village blacksmith was credited with saving his captain.

According to James Dougall's account of the battle, only one militiaman—a man named Nantais—died in the shootout with Putnam's men: "He was shot in the pursuit back in the fields near the woods by a man from behind a fence, who was in turn shot by Nantais' companion, Charlie Lapan." Dougall also credited Lapan as the man who killed Putnam.

When General Putnam's surviving men broke and ran, the Battle of Windsor ended, and with it, the last invasion of the Patriot War sanctioned by the Hunter or Patriot executive.

At about 11:00 a.m., one hundred regulars from the Thirty-fourth Regiment, an artillery crew and fifty Native warriors under Captain Edward Broderick arrived from Fort Malden. By the early afternoon, the full defense force of four hundred had secured the entire Detroit River shore and captured more Hunters.

Twenty-one Hunters and Patriots died in the battle, and Colonel Prince executed five others on the battlefield. Within three days, search parties arrested forty-five prisoners, who were chained and sent on a journey to London, Ontario, to face trial.

Of the scores of men who joined General Bierce in the Windsor raid, the Canadian defenders killed or captured half.

LAST STAND OF COLONEL HARVELL

Several participants in the Battle of Windsor provided personal accounts in memoirs or historical letters of the last moments of the rebel Colonel Harvell. The facts vary dramatically depending on which side of the battle the observer stood and on how much time elapsed since the event. In several cases, the accounts were written decades after the fact.

Everyone seems to agree that Harvell was from Kentucky and was tall (over six feet) and good looking. No one seems to remember his first name. All accounts agree that he died in Baby's orchard, and most say he fell holding aloft the rebel flag. (A remnant of that flag is among the exhibits at the Fort Malden Museum in Amherstburg, Ontario.) Following are several accounts in chronological order.

Journalist Henry C. Grant, who never bothered to learn Harvell's name, reported the story in the December 11, 1838 issue of his newspaper, making his the first account:

> *A printer of Detroit, whose name we could not ascertain, bearing a tri-colored flag fell in the rear of his absconding companions and was immediately shot dead by some of our party. The furled banner he bore was stained with his blood when taken from his stiffened grasp.*

Based on second-hand accounts, Donald McLeod described Harvell's last stand in his 1841 memoirs:

> *When the savage volunteers called upon him to surrender, he declared that there was no such word in the Patriot service and defended himself with a large bowie knife to the very last.*

Robert Marsh gave a highly fictionalized version in 1847:

> *Soon after the battle, he was surrounded by eighteen or twenty and commanded to surrender. "What will be done with me if I do?" said he. "You will be shot immediately on being brought before Col. Prince." "Then," says he, "I may as well die here!" He was a Kentuckian, stood six foot two inches, and large in proportion; he went at them, killed three and wounded four others, before they succeeded in pinning him to the ground with their bayonets. He was killed, however, on the spot, fought to the last with determined fury, with a large bowie knife.*

Jedediah Hunt wrote the following in 1853:

Col. Harvell, finding all attempts futile to stop the fugitive Patriots, confronted three of the regulars single-handed with his long saber, or it was a sort of bowie knife, and mortally wounded two but was finally overcome by being pierced with two musket balls and then bayoneted.

Windsor resident James Dougall stood with the defenders in the orchard. He related the Harvell story this way in an 1885 letter to the *Detroit Free Press*:

One man carried a very large flag, which trailed behind him on the ground. He ran fast, considering the encumbrance of the flag. In the excitement of the moment, I called out, "A hundred dollars to whoever shoots the standard-bearer." He fell immediately after that, pierced by several bullets. He had not time to kneel down, load and fire several shots, or draw a knife.

The last sentence is a purposeful rebuttal to versions of the story told by McLeod and others.

Samuel Lane reflected a dramatic view common among several later chroniclers when he wrote the following in 1892:

Col. Harvell, a large framed, fine-looking Kentuckian, was evidently endeavoring, with the Patriot flag in his hand, to lead the command in a hopeless retreat. Being wounded in the leg, the brave Kentuckian faced about and commenced firing at his pursuers, and when his ammunition was exhausted, still defiantly brandished his bowie knife at them, until finally shot down in his tracks.

Historian Frederick Neal embellished Dougall's version of the story in his 1909 history of Sandwich. In the biography of townsman Pierre Marentette, he wrote:

Capt. Marentette's military life was full of brave and daring deeds. At the battle of Windsor on the 4th of December 1838, it was he who shot the man carrying the rebel flag. James Dougall, who had offered $25 in gold to anyone who would shoot the rebel flag man, came to Sandwich the same afternoon and tendered the money to Mr. Marentette. Mr. Marentette declined to take the reward, saying, "I am not fighting for money. I am fighting for my country."

THE INVADERS FLEE

When General Bierce and his company arrived at the spot where they had left the steamer, the *Champlain* had departed. The now-frantic rebels scoured the shore in every direction for canoes, scows and other small craft. They succeeded in finding enough, and most paddled to safety.

According to Robert Marsh and Jedediah Hunt, bands of Patriots and Hunters fleeing the orchard debacle gathered in the forests outside of Windsor. Marsh wrote:

> *As many of us as could get together after reaching the woods called a council of war, and after consulting together sometime, came to the conclusion that we had been betrayed and that it was useless to attempt to renew the attack. Some, however, were determined to do so, but the majority ruled, and it was finally concluded best for every man to do the best he could for himself.*

In defeat, they fled into the wintry countryside. In singles, pairs and small groups, they headed north, east and south. Most avoided the river, as Marsh explained:

> *Some may ask, "Why did you not make a forced march to the river, take boats and cross over?" To this I must reply, it was talked of, but our force, at that time, was not sufficient to ensure success. Some thought the woods being very extensive, and supposing there were many Patriots living in that district, that we might finally the most, or all of us, succeed in evading their search and in time reach a place of safety.*

Some men did try to cross the river. North of Windsor, several chroniclers claim that the British regulars spotted a canoe with six suspected raiders hurrying across to Detroit. The artillery under command of Lieutenant Dionysius Airey fired at the small vessel. William Baby later recounted, "Some capital shots were made, but without effect until Lieut. Airey himself pointed the gun, when one shot struck the canoe amidships, just as it reached ice, and killed one man and severely wounded another."

Rebels who fled into the countryside eventually needed shelter and food. Timidly, they approached farms seeking help. In several cases, the farmers arrested them at the point of a gun. In other cases, residents provided shelter and aided their escape.

Marsh evaded capture the day of the battle. On December 5, hungry, he inquired at a farm about purchasing food. The French-Canadian loyalist farmer bound Marsh and took him to Sandwich. Joshua Doan fell into custody in a similar manner and found himself manacled to Marsh.

Samuel Snow and two others headed north and walked along the icy shore of Lake St. Clair. The lower section of the lake was still open. Snow and his friends attempted to take the ferry across, but the ferryman refused—he was under orders. Snow's party then headed east and met up with a larger group of their comrades, including Elijah Woodman. All were jailed shortly after arrival in Chatham.

One Western District resident spotted Harrison Goodrich and Cornelius Cunningham trying to arrange passage across Lake St. Clair. He rounded up other loyalists and arrested the two fugitives.

Some rebels did manage to cross Lake St. Clair on the ice. They hid in barn lofts and garrets owned by sympathizers until the lake froze solid, at which point they walked home. Among them was Jedediah Hunt. Others were smuggled to Detroit in hay wagons.

Some rebels died of exposure in the woods. James Dougall reported that searchers found two men frozen at the base of a tree.

Battlefield Executions

By the time Colonel John Prince arrived from Sandwich with four militia companies, nothing remained of the battle but smoke and casualties. Upon hearing of his friend Dr. Hume's murder and the assault on the barracks, Colonel Prince began a ruthless campaign of summary justice. The colonel had openly complained in the previous months about the light treatment of Patriots captured at Fort Malden and Pelee Island early in the year. Few had been tried, some had been released and none had hanged. In Colonel Prince's mind, the invaders held the low status of pirates. His new mantra was "not again."

What follows is evidence given at an inquiry into the battle and later repeated in the British House of Lords (documented in Hansard), with additional details added by William Baby and Donald McLeod.

Lieutenant Benjamin Cheeseman of the Second Essex militia brought forward a prisoner whom he had taken. He surrendered him to Colonel Prince, who ordered him to be shot upon the spot.

A local resident, Charles E. Anderson, dragged a second prisoner, a jeweler from Detroit named Uri Bennett, before Prince. Anderson suspected that Bennett aided in Dr. Hume's murder. The colonel ordered the prisoner taken behind a tavern and shot. Bennett lunged at Anderson. He pushed Bennett aside and suggested he run for his life. Bennett took off across a field behind the tavern.

Colonel William Elliott of the Second Essex militia watched the drama from the tavern balcony. He exclaimed, "Damn you, you cowardly rascals, are you going to murder your prisoner?" His next remark he aimed directly at his son-in-law, Charles Anderson: "Aren't you ashamed at shooting at an unarmed man?"

For a moment, the colonel's remarks retarded the fire of the party, but in the next instant, the prisoner was shot down. Anderson bragged that he blew out Bennett's brains just to make sure he was dead.

Like many in Windsor that day, William Baby disapproved of the executions. He later wrote:

> *It is to be regretted that this painful affair took place in our most public street, and in the presence of several ladies and children, who had been attracted to the doors and windows by the strange events of the morning but who little expected to witness so awful a tragedy.*

Baby also provided details of the next two executions:

> *Another brigand named Dennison, also wounded and unarmed, was taken after the action and brought in during the course of the morning. Charles Elliott, Esq., who happened to be present when the prisoner was about to be shot by Col. Prince's orders, entreated that he might be saved to be dealt with according to the laws of the country; but Col. Prince's reply was, "Damn the rascal, shoot him," and it was done accordingly.*

The shooter was none other than Charles Anderson.

> *When Col. Prince reached Windsor, he was informed that one of the brigands was lying wounded in the house of Mr. Wm. Johnson. The man, whose leg had been shattered by a musket ball, had been found by Francois Baby, Esq., after the action, and by his orders was removed to Mr. Johnson's, with a promise of surgical assistance. Col. Prince gave the order for his execution, and he was dragged out of the house and shot accordingly.*

McLeod names the fourth executed prisoner as Stephen Miller. He was first bayoneted and then shot by Anderson for good measure.

In his written account of the battle, James Dougall displayed remorse for the execution of Miller:

> One poor old man I greatly pitied. He was a farmer from back of Detroit, who had come into the city that day and put up at the Steamboat Hotel, the headquarters of the rebels and patriots. He had got drunk and was induced to go aboard the steamboat. He sobered by the time the boat landed and wished to go back, but could not. He was badly wounded at the battle. Col. Baby and Mr. Johnson, a teacher, hearing his piteous tale, had compassion on him, took him into Johnson's house and bandaged his wounds. Some hours afterwards, he was dragged out and bayoneted.

The Thirty-fourth Regiment, newly arrived from Fort Malden, captured another wounded raider near the river shore. The man appealed for mercy to his captor, Captain Edward Broderick. Broderick assuaged the prisoner's fears when he replied, "You have fallen into the hands of a British officer." However, any quarter given by Broderick evaporated after he left that prisoner under guard in a windmill.

Colonel Prince and his entourage rode to the windmills and met the men attending Broderick's prisoner. He ordered the man to be taken from the guard and shot upon the spot. Charles Anderson, while astride his horse, happily obliged.

"The Prince of Monsters," as Donald McLeod later called Colonel Prince, seemed prepared to shoot every prisoner he encountered that day. According to Baby, the serial executions ended only when the colonel was shamed by a group of twenty Huron and Chippewa warriors who had joined the search. Baby wrote:

> The Indians had taken seven prisoners, and one or two of them proposed that they should be shot; but one of their chiefs said, "No, we are Christians. We will not murder them—we will deliver them to our officers to be treated as they think proper." They were then brought to Col. Prince, who had now commenced his return to Sandwich. When he had arrived opposite the burning barracks, he ordered the wagon in which the prisoners had been placed to be wheeled off the road. As soon as it had reached an open spot in the rear of the ruins, he commanded the men be taken out and shot. At this critical moment, Charles Elliott and Robert Mercer, Esqs., and the

Rev. Mr. Johnson and Mr. Samuel James rushed forward and entreated Col. Prince not to commit murder by shooting the prisoners, but begged him to leave them to the laws of the country. In making this appeal, Mr. James made use of the emphatic language: "For God's sake, do not let a white man murder what an Indian has spared." Col. Prince yielded to the entreaties of the gentlemen, remarking to Mr. Elliott that he would hold him responsible for his interference, as his orders were to destroy them all.

Colonel Prince's battlefield executions did not go unchallenged. Local citizens complained to the government. The summary executions at Windsor shocked Sir George Arthur. He believed Colonel Prince's lust for revenge diverted his attentions from his real duty of pursuing the Patriots after their defeat. Sir George also feared the incident could have sparked war between Great Britain and the United States.

Colonel Prince faced a court of inquiry in February 1839, but he remained widely popular in Upper Canada for his rough justice. In a classic case of the victors make the rules, the court of inquiry ultimately exonerated him on March 14. The Upper Canada government, which abhorred his methods, liked the results. The Hunter assaults ceased.

In the House of Lords, Henry Peter Brougham, 1st Baron Brougham and Vaux, later argued that Prince's actions could be judged only as murder:

Suppose a man who had shot another was pointed out to him an hour after, and that he then put the murderer to death, he should himself be guilty of murder. Even if he saw a murder committed, and put the murderer to death, he should be guilty of murder, unless it was done in self-defence. Suppose even that he saw a man convicted after a trial by a jury of his peers and sentenced to die—nay, suppose him outside the prison door on his way to the place of execution, and that he should then destroy him—even in this case, and their Lordships would admit it was a strong one, he should be guilty of murder. This was the law.

Colonel Prince never expressed remorse for his battlefield murders. In fact, he later stated his "deep regret that he did not shoot every scoundrel of them as fast as he was brought in."

Chapter 11

Prisoners Tried and Executed: January 1839

The colonial government had shown significant restraint in punishing prisoners captured during raids from Michigan and Ohio in early 1838, but that changed by the fall. By the end of 1838, Upper Canada's lieutenant governor, Sir George Arthur, had already approved executions by hanging of nine Patriot rebels captured during attacks in the Lake Ontario and St. Lawrence River area. Prisoners captured after the Battle of Windsor were next.

TRIALS OF WINDSOR CAPTIVES

Those captured after the Windsor battle spent months imprisoned in vile quarters before and after their trials. Marsh's book goes into excruciating detail about their deplorable conditions. The cells were unheated—Marsh and Woodman suffered frost damage to their feet. There was not enough room for all men to sleep at the same time. Lice and other vermin infested the cells, and the food was limited and coarse. Marsh notes that the officers tended to be tyrants but that the ranks often showed pity and provided bits of extra food.

Snow waited for trial in the same jail as Marsh. He never complained about the vermin and unheated cells, but he did remark on the unwholesome nature of their food.

The 1834 courthouse where Patriot rebels were tried and hanged stands majestically in central London, Ontario. *Photo by the author*.

The trials of the forty-five Hunters and Patriots captured after the battle began less than four weeks later. Each man faced a court-martial in London, Upper Canada, under the Lawless Aggressions Act. Convictions were almost guaranteed and hanging a likely result.

The judge advocate for the London court-martial was Henry Sherwood. Sherwood, thirty-one, was a tightly connected member of the Family Compact, the cabal of elites that ran Upper Canada and provided the catalyst for the rebellion, and was related to Solicitor General Henry John Boulton. Sherwood also sat in the colonial assembly, being first elected in 1836. When William Lyon Mackenzie and his ill-prepared band of rebels marched on Toronto in December 1837, Sherwood was in the defense force that defeated the rebels north of the city.

Sherwood used the trial of rebel officer Hiram Lynn as an example of how to properly apply the law. He went methodically through the evidence and explained and proved the three facts required under the Lawless Aggressions Act as it applied to the American prisoners: that the prisoner was a citizen of a foreign country at peace with Britain, that the prisoner

119

conspired with British subjects and that the prisoner actively bore arms on British soil against loyal subjects of Her Majesty Queen Victoria.

Sherwood court-martialed all Windsor prisoners between December 27, 1838, and January 18, 1839. He tried the rebel officers singly and the ranks in groups. Five of the Windsor prisoners—David McDougall, Daniel Sweetman, George Putnam, Sidney Barber and William Bartlett—became witnesses for the prosecution in exchange for a promise of mercy.

Sherwood took the most conservative interpretation of the act possible and kept a tight rein on the London proceedings. He insisted that the prisoners' statements to the court be written in advance and read by him. He did not let prisoners question witnesses directly. Sherwood cross-examined witnesses on behalf of the prisoners, thus being at times the prosecutor and the defense counsel.

Snow later wrote about the hopelessness of their position:

> *Three, four, and half a dozen at a time, were called up before the judge advocate, where the witnesses for the Crown were waiting to convict whom they pleased. The prisoners were not permitted to interrogate the witnesses, but the questions we wished to ask must be given to the judge, and he would put them to the witnesses in the shape that suited him best.*

Many London prisoners stated in their defense that they were coerced or misled and had not meant to fight. That defense was worthless. The men had been caught bearing arms "against the Queen," and that was all that mattered.

Robert Marsh faced the court-martial on the next to last day in a group of six. He wrote that George Putnam fingered him as being in the battle, claiming that Marsh was a lieutenant.

Elijah Woodman and Chauncey Sheldon, at forty-two and fifty-seven, respectively, were among the oldest prisoners. Their trial, on January 18, 1839, was the last. Woodman wrote that on the night before, both had been given a document of evidence against them and had only a few hours to prepare a defense.

Woodman called Marsh as a defense witness. Marsh confirmed that Woodman had criticized the invasion plans while in Michigan, for which Colonel Harvell had chastised him. Woodman claimed officers told the men on the steamer that they were going to Black River in Michigan, not to Windsor. Woodman had business with a man at Black River and thus boarded the steamer. Daniel Sweetman, George Putnam and David

McDougall testified against him. The court-martial pronounced him guilty and sentenced him to hang.

In the end, forty-four men were convicted and thirty-eight sentenced to death. Only Abraham Tiffany was acquitted. The state produced no evidence against him, and Sherwood later wrote the court believed him to be insane.

Ultimately, in April 1839, the court discharged and deported the five turncoat witnesses and fifteen other captives: Robert Whitney, Orin J.S. Mabee, Joseph Grason, Stephen Meadow, Harrison P. Goodrich, John Charter Williams, Daniel Kennedy, Joseph Horton, Ezra Horton, Cornelius Higgins, Charles Reed, David Hay, William Jones, Israel Gibbs Attwood and Trueman Woodbury. Woodbury, taking no chances, escaped before the order arrived.

The final resolution of the forty-five men captured for invading Windsor was: one acquitted, twenty guilty but discharged, eighteen guilty and sentenced to transport for life and six guilty and condemned to hang. Snow wrote, "After the trials were concluded, they commenced picking out the fat sheep for hanging. Those who had held military office in the Patriot service come under this head."

The executions began before the trials were completed.

WINDSOR PRISONERS EXECUTED

Hiram Benjamin Lynn, twenty-six, was the first to fall through the scaffold's trap door. A resident of Ann Arbor, Michigan, he served as an adjutant in the Patriot army and was wounded in battle. According to a letter from an acquaintance, Hiram "was orphaned early in life, raised himself, and developed sympathy for the oppressed." As a rebel leader accused of leading the bloody assault on the Windsor barracks, he was hanged on January 7, 1839.

Lieutenant Governor George Arthur had expected thousands of spectators to show support for the government by coming to view the execution of Lynn and other rebels. He misjudged the temper of the London-area residents. While the majority did not condone the raids, they sympathized with the rebel cause. Only an estimated two hundred people viewed Lynn's hanging.

On January 11, Canadian Daniel Davis Bedford, twenty-seven, died. Bedford, a former innkeeper from the village of Norwich and a father of three, was a committed rebel. He'd marched with Dr. Charles Duncombe in

Daniel Bedford's barely legible gravestone stands in the old Quaker cemetery in Norwich, Ontario. *Photo by the author.*

the aborted rebellion in the London district the previous December. He was captured as Dr. Duncombe's army fled but was granted bail. He absconded to America, where he joined the Patriot army.

A young American from New Hampshire, Albert Clark, twenty-one, was hanged on January 14.

American-born Cornelius Cunningham, thirty-two, had resided in Upper Canada for eight years. He worked as a wagon maker in the village of Beachville near present-day Woodstock, Ontario. He held the rank of colonel among the Patriot raiders. The British policy was to hang officers, and Cunningham met his fate on February 4. His final words were: "Let it be remembered that I died a martyr in the cause of liberty."

Amos Perley, a young Canadian originally from New Brunswick, had long resided in the United States. He joined the Patriots to help liberate his fellow Canadians and rose to the rank of major. One of the men in the jury that convicted Amos was his cousin, Charles Strange Perley. Amos hanged on February 6, 1839, and sprang "into eternity, without a struggle," according to one newspaper report.

On the gallows that day with Perley was Joshua Doan, twenty-eight. He and his brother Joel were both caught up in the reform movement led by Dr. Duncombe. After the uprising in December 1837, Joshua and Joel fled to the United States. Joel stayed out of trouble. Joshua didn't.

Joshua's last letter to his wife, Fanny, has survived for posterity:

London, January 27ᵗʰ, 1839

Dear Wife,

I am at this moment confined in the cell from which I am to go to the scaffold. I received my sentence today, and am to be executed on February 6ᵗʰ. I am permitted to see you tomorrow any time after 10 o'clock in the morning, as may suit you best. I wish you to think of such questions as you wish to ask me, as I do not know how long you will be permitted to stay. Think as little of my unhappy fate as you can; as from the love you bear me, I know too well how it must affect you. I wish you to inform my father and brother of my sentence as soon as possible. I must say good-bye for the night, and may God protect you and my dear child, and give you fortitude to meet that coming event with the Christian grace and fortitude which is the gift of Him, our Lord, who created us. That this may be the case is the prayer of your affectionate husband,

JOSHUA G. DOANE

At their final meeting, Fanny had to be torn from her husband's arms by jail guards. (She later married Joshua's brother Joel.) The modern town of Sparta, Ontario, exists as a few houses at a crossroad. West of Sparta is the old Quaker cemetery. In it lie the graves of Joshua Doan and Amos Perley.

While it was the intent of the colonial government to make an example, the crowds at the public executions remained smaller and less enthusiastic than had been the case with the hangings in Kingston and Toronto. "A reason given for these executions is that the loyal portion of the country

Joshua Doan's grave stands in the old Quaker cemetery west of Sparta, Ontario. *Photo by the author.*

requires satisfaction for the injuries they have received," wrote Scotland-born pioneer Presbyterian clergyman Dr. William Proudfoot (1788–1851). "What a savage set of beings these loyalists must be! Now what satisfaction can it give any man to see a man hanged; who but a devil would derive any satisfaction from such a scene?"

By the time Doan and Perley died, the mood of London-area residents had gone from somber to angry. That public discontent may have saved other men from the noose. The barbarism of the public hangings did not dissipate quickly. Several historians report that dozens of reform-oriented families, especially those with American roots, sold their Canadian holdings and moved from western Upper Canada to the United States in 1839 and 1840.

Chapter 12

Upper Canada Releases Selected Prisoners: 1839–40

I n February 1839, Upper Canada hanged its last Patriot or Hunter raider. That dubious honor went to Lyman Leach, forty, from Salina, New York, captured at the Battle of the Windmill in November 1838.

In the spring of 1839, colonial jails still held western Patriots captured at the attack on Fort Malden in January 1838, the occupation of Pelee Island in March 1838 and the Battle of Windsor in December 1838. Jails and prisons also held scores of men captured in Patriot raids on eastern Upper Canada.

With the last hanging behind him, Sir George Arthur began to implement a policy of repatriation for convicted American Patriot and Hunter prisoners, especially the youngest.

On April 8, 1839, Sir George released twenty-two prisoners, mostly teens and young men, held at Fort Henry for participating in the Battle of the Windmill. Their chartered steamer arrived at Sackets Harbor, New York, to cheering friends and family. On April 27, thirty-seven more pardoned men landed at Sackets Harbor to adoring crowds.

RELEASE OF THELLER'S CREW

The seven remaining men captured with Dr. Theller on the *Anne* or recaptured after the big escape in Quebec—Theron R. Culver, Henry Hull, Abraham W. Partridge, Benjamin Pew, Chauncey Parker, Squire Thayer and Nathaniel Smith—still resided in the Citadel, as did Thomas Jefferson Sutherland. These prisoners presented the colonial government with a dilemma. Thanks to the successful defense presented by Sutherland at his trial, none of the *Anne* captives could be tried under the Lawless Aggressions Act because their crimes occurred before the act existed. As Americans, they could not be tried for treason. No Canadian died in the Amherstburg raid, and no buildings burned, so a murder or arson charge would not stand. Keeping them in prison further without a trial served no purpose.

In the end, an Upper Canada sheriff, Alexander McMartin, escorted the seven remaining *Anne* captives to the border at St. Regis, Quebec, in May 1839 and turned them over to a minor American functionary named Heman W. Tucker. American newspapers widely reported that Tucker dressed down the Canadian sheriff with pointed complaints about British tyranny and mistreatment of prisoners. His remarks backfired.

According the memoirs of Hunter captain Daniel D. Heustis, a captive at Fort Henry, a list existed in May 1839 naming twenty-five additional men due for pardons. When the Upper Canada populace heard about Tucker's inflammatory words, citizen anger and resentment made it politically impossible for Sir George to continue being lenient. He shut the door to further repatriation. Heustis claimed his name was on that last list.

Sutherland Set Free

Thomas Jefferson Sutherland had his original death sentence commuted to transport in 1838. As he waited in the dreary Citadel, he worked for his freedom. An experienced writer with a sound knowledge of law, Sutherland sent a lengthy letter to Lord Durham, Canada's governor general, dated July 4, 1838, detailing the legal errors in his case.

Six weeks later, Lord Durham set aside the guilty verdict due to its legal irregularities. Durham told Sutherland in writing that he could return to America if he posted a $4,000 bond to ensure he would stay off British soil.

Sutherland then protested by letter to Lord Glenelg, secretary of state for the colonies, that he could not raise bail while in prison in a city where he knew no one. He questioned the flawed logic of the order, which required him to get bail in Canada and then leave never to return. What bailsman would agree to that arrangement? In the end, the colonial boss saw his logic and set in motion his repatriation.

Sutherland traveled with the *Anne* captives from the Citadel in May 1839, but the sheriff did not hand him over at St. Regis, apparently because the paperwork for his release was not in order. Instead, the sheriff presented Sutherland to authorities on the American side of the St. Lawrence River opposite Cornwall a few days later.

Sutherland immediately looked up his old rebel comrades, including Donald McLeod and Benjamin Lett, but not Dr. Edward Theller. If Sutherland harbored dreams of new battles, they were futile. The Patriot War's military activity had passed, never to be rekindled.

RELEASE OF PELEE ISLAND PRISONERS

In 1839, the ten surviving prisoners from the Pelee Island occupation— Philip Jackson, Diogenes Mackenzie, Benjamin Warner, Isaac Mace, John McIntyre, Samuel Wood, William Carroll, Isaac Myers, Philip Brady and William McCarrick—resided in Fort Henry, Kingston, with scores of other captives from various battles.

While the crimes of the Pelee Island prisoners occurred after the Lawless Aggressions Act was enacted, an odd technical difficulty arose at the July 1839 trial of Jackson, Mackenzie, Warner, Mace and McIntyre. Two captives, William Carroll, eighteen, and Samuel Wood, forty-four, agreed to give testimony in exchange for a reduced sentence. Carroll turned out to be the only British subject among the ten.

Justice James Buchanan Macaulay presided at the trial. George Rideout represented the five accused on trial. He proposed a very restrictive view of the wording of the Lawless Aggressions Act, and he strenuously argued that the act required the American raiders to be joined by British subjects in the plural—that is, that the single British subject, Carroll, was not enough. Rideout cited a legal case in which a man who stole one horse was acquitted because the statute referred to stealing horses. Macaulay rejected the singular interpretation.

The jury returned a guilty verdict; however, Rideout had planted seeds of doubt in the magistrate's mind, and Macaulay consulted others about the singular interpretation. He received opposing opinions. He then waited for the return of Upper Canada Chief Justice John Beverley Robinson, who was away in England defending the Lawless Aggressions Act before his masters. In the meantime, the prisoners counted the passing weeks and months in their cells and watched as the ranks of Patriot prisoners dwindled until only they remained.

In 1840, the government repealed the Lawless Aggressions Act for several months before enacting a stronger version. In that gap, Upper Canada released Carroll and conveyed the nine American prisoners to the border and banished them for life.

Considering that the Pelee Island battle accounted for the second largest casualty list the British incurred in the Patriot War, the fact that none of the American prisoners hanged seems a miracle, though it may be a case of public hanging fatigue.

Chapter 13

Rebellion Fades: 1839–40

After the Windsor debacle, Lucius Verus Bierce stepped down as top commander of the Hunters. He was twice indicted in U.S. courts for violation of the neutrality laws, but the matter was dropped, and he resumed his law practice in Akron.

General Henry S. Handy resumed control in the west, while General Donald McLeod maintained control in the east. Those two men clearly did not know they'd lost the war.

On assuming command, General Handy asked General McLeod to come out west (meaning the Chicago area) and prepare men for the Patriot cause. He did. In his report delivered to General Handy in April or May 1839, General McLeod claimed to have ready "3,250 efficient men ready for service when called for." These troops included 1,500 Native warriors, many groups of Americans and two companies of French Canadians. General Handy, too, claimed to have armies of Native warriors in America and Canada ready to fight, if paid for it. He also claimed that one or two score of small cannon were ready to be cast in Detroit.

Despite claims by Generals McLeod and Handy to the contrary, no evidence shows that Native Americans were ready to risk their lives in a white man's war.

Canada's aboriginal warriors certainly would not join the rebels. They supported Britain in the Patriot War as they had during the War of 1812. Warriors accompanied militia units and regular forces during suppression of Dr. Duncombe's uprising, the Battle of Pelee Island, the St. Clair River raids and the Battle of Windsor.

The claims by the two generals were all blather. By the time General McLeod delivered his report to General Handy, stocks of weapons were in short supply because of insufficient funds. Sympathizers who once donated money to the Hunters had begun to fade in number and generosity. A handful of prominent men retained executive positions, and hardcore groups of fighters remained on the ready, but after a dozen failed invasions of Canada from Michigan to Vermont in 1838, everyone knew Upper Canada was unassailable by a citizen army.

The Patriot and Hunters invasions had put the colony on full war alert. By the end of 1838, Britain had rebuilt old forts, such as Fort Malden, and added to its infantry and artillery.

Britain had 12,000 regulars stationed in the Canadian colonies. Upper Canada could call on support from an active militia of 21,000, plus over 200,000 inactive militiamen that could be mobilized in a few days. Canada had a big enough defensive force in 1839 to repel any invasion from America, be it an unsanctioned civilian army or the military might of the United States.

Hunters Contemplate Another Raid on Windsor

The Hunters Lodge popularity peaked in the spring of 1839 and then slowly receded. Repeated military failures in 1838 combined with aggressive enforcement of the U.S. neutrality law along the border dampened enthusiasm. Also, the new governor general of Canada, Lord Durham, presented a report to his British bosses in February 1839 that called for political reform in the colonies. With bloodless reform a possibility, fewer men felt a need to risk their life and liberty.

Instead of full-scale invasions, Hunter strategy switched to guerrilla-style raids into Canada. The raiders torched the barns and crops of men known to be ardent government supporters. In 1839, Britain and America were noisily disputing the boundary between Maine and New Brunswick, and war seemed possible. The Hunters hoped their nuisance raids would add fuel to the fire. Nothing came of it—both countries settled peacefully.

On September 18, 1839, eighteen or nineteen senior delegates from the Hunters Lodge met at Lockport, New York, "to consult upon the plan that should be adopted by the Patriots to carry their wishes into effect."

Delegates from the Canadian lodges stated, according to Buffalo historian Orrin Tiffany, that when the next attack upon Canada happened, seven hundred men could be furnished. The American delegates claimed they had three thousand men capable of invasion, with stands of arms in Buffalo and Detroit, including cannon. The convention concluded by deciding to invade Upper Canada again at Windsor. Reports stated that General Donald McLeod and Thomas Jefferson Sutherland were ready to depart to Detroit to make preparations.

A subsequent meeting in October in Lewiston, New York, reversed that decision. The delegates, including General McLeod, Sutherland and Benjamin Lett, agreed to forego an invasion of Canada until Canadians showed a willingness to rise up in defense of their own liberty.

In reality, no large body of men could be found who were ready to engage the now beefed-up armed forces in Upper Canada.

Beset by fading popularity and an expanding controversy about misuse of donated money, the Hunters Lodge ceased to be a military threat by 1840. It did retain enough political clout to shape state and national elections in 1840. Hunters and Patriots helped dash President Van Buren's hope for a second term.

MACKENZIE'S LAST PATRIOT HURRAH

William Lyon Mackenzie came to realize that Canada's liberation could not come from America. On March 22, 1839, he held a convention in Rochester, New York, to discuss Canada's independence. In the end, the fifty Patriot leaders in attendance formed yet another society, the Association of Canadian Refugees (ACR), with John Montgomery as president. As part of its founding charter, the group pledged to prevent further "hasty and ill-prepared expeditions or attacks" on Canada. The aim was to aid Canadians in any internal uprising but not to sanction further raids by Americans.

In contrast to the Hunter Lodge leadership, which was American dominated, Mackenzie's Rochester association and its auxiliary branch in Cincinnati, Ohio, extended membership to Canadians only.

In May 1839, General Handy requested that the ACR join in a new endeavor. General Handy wanted to unite the dissidents in Upper and Lower Canada under one banner "as did the thirteen United States during the Revolution." Mackenzie did not respond to the request—he was then imprisoned for breaching the neutrality laws.

Under Montgomery's leadership, General Handy's suggestion seems to have been tried. In January 1840, police arrested two men in Toronto for trying to recruit volunteers for the Upper Canada Patriot army. The idea never gained support in Canada and faded away.

THE FIRST CASUALTY

The first casualty of war is truth, or so sages have said, beginning with Aeschylus in about 500 BC. The Patriot War was no different.

Throughout the conflict, supporters of both sides exaggerated the number of men they fought against, the number of opponents killed and the elapsed time for any battle. In order to garner support for their cause and to vilify the other, both sides claimed that the enemy committed various atrocities.

In the Patriot War, dead cabin boys and mutilated officers were the popular propaganda tactics.

In Dr. Edward Theller's account of the capture of the schooner *Anne*, he included this detail: "A little boy, a Canadian refugee, engaged in bringing us loaded muskets was killed in the act, fell overboard, and his body found on shore the next morning."

Since Dr. Theller never saw the shore the next morning, who told him? And why did no one else, such as William Baby, mention such a tragedy?

In his second deposition, Gilman Appleby added the following segment, absent in his first deposition:

> That deponent had a boy with him on board said boat who was usually called "Little Billy" and who had formerly been with the deponent on the lake in the Constitution *steamboat; and that this boy was shot in the storehouse door, and fell into the river; and deponent has not been able to hear of him since that time.*

Why would Captain Appleby forget such a sad story the first time? Or was he just trying to manufacture more outrage, since people had begun to doubt his story about people perishing on the *Caroline* as it tipped over the great falls?

There is no corroborative information to support either claim of the nearly anonymous dead boy.

British sources claimed that the Windsor invaders mutilated Dr. Hume's body with an axe after his death. After the Battle of the Windmill, the British (and many later historians) insisted that the Hunter raiders there mutilated the body of Lieutenant William Johnson. In both cases, free-roaming hogs were present. Voracious swine were likely the culprits.

Chapter 14

Transported to Van Diemen's Land: 1839–50

This chapter blends the experiences of transported raiders from both the western and eastern fronts of the Patriot War. Once in Van Diemen's Land, the exiled Canadians and Americans worked in the same road gangs. They traveled in groups when looking for work as ticket-of-leave men, they combined resources to get passage home and they generally helped one another. Their stories and fates intermingle.

Seven of the exiled Patriots and Hunters who returned from transport to Van Diemen's Land—William Gates, Daniel Heustis, Robert Marsh, Linus Miller, Samuel Snow, Benjamin Wait and Stephen Wright—wrote detailed memoirs and observations. None were ashamed of their actions, and all wanted the sacrifice of their comrades remembered. An eighth book, which included first-hand accounts by Elijah Woodman, appeared long after his death. Together, their accounts tell a compelling story of hardship, courage, stamina and hope.

Shipping Out

The prisoners transported to Van Diemen's Land for participating in the Short Hills raid in June 1838 were the first shipped out. In their case, they stopped in England to await a southbound ship. After a miserable few months either in Newgate Prison or a prison hulk anchored in the Portsmouth

These upper and lower casements at Fort Henry housed Patriot captives pending trial or shipment to penal colonies. *Photo by the author.*

harbor, they continued on in two groups. The *Marquis of Hastings* set sail from Portsmouth, England, on March 16, 1839, with ten rebels, while the *Canton* departed London, England, on September 22, 1839, with three. Both ships also carried over two hundred common criminals. The remainder of the Patriot and Hunter prisoners sailed to Van Diemen's Land on the *Buffalo*.

On September 23, 1839, blacksmiths arrived at Fort Henry in Kingston just after breakfast. They chained the condemned transportees in twos at their wrists and ankles. This included sixty prisoners captured at the Battle of the Windmill, eighteen men from the Battle of Windsor and one man from the St. Clair River raids.

In pairs, the men, mostly Americans, marched from the fort between lines of soldiers to a canal boat waiting in the bay. As soon as guards secured them in the hold, they set out. A small steamer towed them up the Rideau Canal from Kingston to Ottawa and then down the Ottawa River to Montreal.

In Montreal, the captives transferred ships and set out immediately for Quebec City, arriving the next day. In the harbor, an aging seven-hundred-ton British war ship, the *Buffalo*, rode at anchor. The seventy-nine Upper

Canada prisoners joined fifty-eight prisoners from the rebellion in Lower Canada and five common criminals.

The *Buffalo* hoisted its sails on September 28, 1839, and began the nearly five-month voyage to the antipodes with just one stop in Argentina.

Life onboard the convict ships varied with the vessel. On the *Buffalo*, except for an hour or so on deck each day, they lived in cramped quarters too low to stand straight in, without windows and with poor air circulation. Samuel Snow complained about the restricted access to fresh air:

> *During the voyage, we were kept upon the lower deck, with the exception of being allowed once a day to go above for a short time for exercise. This indulgence was not allowed to all at the same time. Generally, four messes of twelve men each were ordered up at a time. After we had traversed the length of the deck a few times, looked out upon the broad ocean, and inhaled a few doses of fresh air, we were again remanded below.*

Prisoners performed daily duties on the *Buffalo*, as described by Daniel Heustis:

> *The prisoners were divided into messes. Each mess consisted of twelve men, who were directed to choose from their own number a captain. I was selected for that office by the ninth mess, and my duty consisted in superintending the labor assigned to my messmates and in the exercise of a general supervision in regard to them. Our platform-deck was holystoned and our quarters cleaned every morning, each mess in its turn performing that duty. Our berth-boards, too, were occasionally whitewashed; but, notwithstanding these salutary regulations, our quarters were infested with vermin, such as cockroaches, fleas, and the like.*

Image of Daniel Heustis, from the cover of his memoirs.

In the tropics, the heat was oppressive. Snow wrote, "We suffered much from heat and thirst while we were sailing between the tropics, and the water on board getting short—we were put upon an allowance of one and a half pints per day."

Food remained a regular complaint. Heustis described weak skilly for breakfast; old, leathery beef and pea soap for lunch; and mystery biscuits and cocoa for supper.

Marsh and Heustis wrote how the captives plotted to take over the *Buffalo* and sail it to an American port. However, two of the common criminals reported the plot to the captain, and any hope of success evaporated.

In comparison, Linus Miller's description of his voyage on the *Canton* makes it seem like a luxury cruise:

> *Two tiers of berths, large enough for five men each, were fitted up on either side, and thirty hammocks were slung at night in the intermediate space. The height between decks was six feet eight inches. Two large hatchways, always kept open but secured with iron bars, ventilated the prison. The floor and berths were clean, and a proper regard to the health of the prisoners appeared to be scrupulously observed.*

Prisoners on the *Canton* were expected to be on deck in good weather three-quarters of the day. Food was also marginally better than it was on other ships, as Miller described:

> *For convenience in rationing, they were divided into twenty-four messes of ten men each. Eleven ounces of ship biscuit of an inferior quality, one half pound of salt meat, one pint of pea soup, or five ounces of a plain suet pudding, one pint of sweetened tea for breakfast, and the same quantity of cocoa for supper, were allowed each man daily. A small quantity of wine, or lime juice, was also served to each man as a preventive to scurvy.*

LIFE IN THE PENAL COLONY

The *Marquis of Hastings* anchored off the colonial capital, Hobart Town (now called Hobart), on July 23, 1839. Benjamin Wait, one of the rebels on board, later wrote that twelve convicts died in the first weeks in the colony from the effects of the voyage. That included three other Short Hills Raiders: John McNulty, Alexander McLeod and Garret Van Camp. Wait spent eight weeks

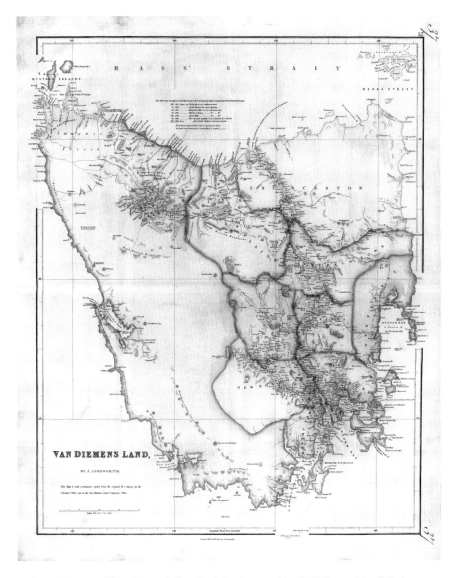

A circa 1834 map of Van Diemen's Land by John Arrowsmith. *David Rumsey Map Collection.*

in the port hospital with a wound so infected that the surgeons considered amputating one arm.

The *Canton* arrived on January 12, 1840. On that ship, Miller said they were under the charge of a naval surgeon, John Irvine, not the captain. Dr. Irvine was to receive one guinea for each man he unloaded alive in Van Diemen's Land and thus took good care of them.

Linus Miller.

The dates of the ship arrivals became significant. Prior to 1840, the penal administrators parceled out new convicts to settlers. The convicts provided free labor in exchange for room and board, so the six Short Hills raiders from the *Marquis of Hastings* who survived had an easier time than their comrades who arrived in 1840. For example, Benjamin Wait and Samuel Chandler found employment on a ranch— Chandler as a carpenter and Wait as clerk and schoolteacher. The other four were George Cooley, James Waggoner, John Vernon and Norman Mallory.

Beginning in 1840, the colony assigned all new convicts to government chain gangs. That fate befell all Patriot and Hunter prisoners transported on the *Buffalo* and *Canton*.

The *Buffalo* dropped anchor in the Hobart Town harbor on February 12, 1840. Its convict passengers also ended the voyage in poor health. One rebel, American Asa Priest, died on the voyage.

The *Buffalo* sailed onto Sydney, Australia, where the fifty-eight Lower Canadians disembarked on February 26. The British later shipped one English-speaking Lower Canada prisoner, Benjamin Mott, back to Van Diemen's Land.

After spending a day on board the *Buffalo* being examined by port health inspectors and cataloged by clerks, the survivors who could walk disembarked. Guards marched the prisoners, weak and stumbling on their sea legs, out of Hobart Town one mile to the Sandy Bay Probation Station. They could be forgiven for assuming they'd crossed the threshold of Hell, as documented by William Gates:

> *We had gone but a short distance when we passed four scaffolds, upon which as many men were just about to be executed. And a little further along, beyond the town, we passed a gang of criminals—some two*

hundred in number—working the road in heavy chains; and yet a little further along was another gang, without the chains. This we thought was an ominous reception.

Prisoners had to turn in their civilian clothing in exchange for prison garb. William Gates wrote:

We now had to exchange our clothing for the convict's suit, which consisted of trousers and jacket, made of a grey kind of cloth, coarser and rougher even than common carpeting, and which permitted the wind to circulate through its interstices almost as freely as through a sieve; a striped cotton shirt whose fabric was correspondingly as coarse; a skull cap made of stiff sole leather, closely fitting the head and projecting in four points from the four sides, which points were so made that they could be turned up or down; and a pair of thick, clumsy shoes, without socks.

Samuel Snow used sarcasm in his clothing description: "At Sandy Bay, we were divested of our threadbare garments and enrobed in nice suits of domestic manufacture, got up after the latest improved convict fashion."

Prisoners capable of standing assembled for an inspection by Sir John Franklin. In 1836, the famous polar explorer became the colony's lieutenant governor, surely one of the least glamorous patronage appointments in the British Empire.

Gates and Robert Marsh wrote that Franklin, in full uniform, lectured them astride a horse, speaking in meandering, unfinished sentences while staring at the sky. The gist of his message: they were very bad men who had committed a horrible crime.

Marsh, in his usual iconoclastic republican style, showed no respect for the colonial governor:

This statue of Sir John Franklin is the centerpiece of Franklin Square near the harbor in Hobart, Tasmania. *Photo by the author.*

"His horse I felt sorry for, standing for nearly two hours, supporting an enormous mass of blubber and wind, weighing I should think, three hundred pounds."

Several of the rebel autobiographers nicknamed Franklin "Old Granny."

Heustis, normally the diplomat among the rebels, resented having to take his hat off for "a servant of royalty" and had little nice to write about their new warden:

> *The Governor was a man of about the ordinary height and of sufficient corpulency to indicate that his own larder was well supplied, whatever might be the fare meted out to the prisoners. A dark complexion, low forehead, dull hazel eyes, and large and prominent nose, mouth, and chin, presented some of the leading features of his countenance, in which it was impossible to discern any indications of superior intellect.*

Franklin also greeted and lectured the other rebel convicts on their arrival. Miller wrote:

> *However starved he might have been as "Captain Franklin" in his northern expedition, he had been more fortunate in the south as governor of the land of Nod, and that here there was no scarcity of grease and good foraging. His countenance, altogether, was rather open, frank and honest; and I was not long in arriving at the conclusion that he was an imbecile old man; a paragon of good nature; with an excellent opinion of himself, and little wit to uphold it.*

As Marsh and other chroniclers noted, Franklin did not know what to do with the Americans. Typical penal convicts were uneducated, British petty criminals. Facing the governor were idealistic men of education and good social standing with no previous criminal record. Franklin stated he would put them on the road gangs and write to England for further instructions.

Guards escorted all prisoners to probation stations (work camps) where, despite their weakened state from the voyage, they were soon subjected to hard labor.

The prison clothes and shoes fell apart in two or three months, according to Heustis, but were replaced only every four to six months. Many worked nearly naked and barefoot for months at a time in all manner of weather. Later, their replacement uniforms were colored half yellow and half black to make their convict status evident at a glace. These were issued by Franklin after an escape from the Lovely Banks Probation Station. Prisoners called the uniforms "magpies" because of how they looked.

On the road gang, the daily food ration per man was meager and often vile, according to all the chroniclers. Heustis wrote:

> *Our food consisted of one pound and five ounces of coarse bread, baked in the most indifferent manner, three fourths of a pound of fresh meat, half a pound of potatoes, and half an ounce of salt, with two ounces of flour for skilly in the morning, and the same at night. This was the daily ration for each man, without variation, from one end of the year to the other. The meat was boiled, or half boiled, and the broth served us for drink. From a pint of this broth, it was frequently no difficult matter to scrape off a spoonful of maggots.*

For two years, they built roads in slave-like conditions, often chained at the ankles. Their captors forced them to push heavy carts laden with rocks without help from horses, mules or other livestock. They became the beasts of burden. Other days, they broke rocks with sledgehammers. At night, they struggled for warmth in thin blankets in simple huts with no fire to heat them, often in wet clothing. James Gemmell wrote, "Although in the prime of life, accustomed to farm work and strong, I have often been weary almost to fainting, and never once in those two tedious years did I go to bed otherwise than hungry."

The hard work, poor housing and inadequate diet took a heavy toll on the health of many. According to various convict accounts, tuberculosis, then called consumption, was rampant. It infected Robert Marsh, Alvin Sweet, Aaron Dresser, Moses Dutcher, Leonard Delano and Daniel Liscombe. Their TB did not kill them, at least not in the penal colony. Others who had TB died, including Thomas Stockton, Elijah Woodman, John McNulty, Alexander McLeod and Andrew Leeper.

The guards usually freed convicts from labor on Saturday afternoons and Sunday. On Saturdays, they washed their clothes and bodies as best they could with their two-ounce ration of soap. On Sundays, Heustis claimed they were forced to attend an Anglican church in the morning, regardless of their religion.

Some men took jobs on weekends on the sly outside of camp in their few spare hours. With their meager earnings, they bought food, soap and tobacco. Men occasionally snared small game and roasted it over a fire, even though that was forbidden.

Men found or made what pleasures they could. Miller wrote:

> *We had worked hard all day in the cold rain, and as usual were locked into our cheerless huts after the day's toil, to sleep in our wet clothing until the morrow should again call us to the performance of our cruel tasks. Suddenly, [Elijah] Woodman sprang from his berth [and began to sing] "Me Hunters of Kentucky." The effect was instantaneous. As if electrified, every man sprang to the floor; sick, blind and halt, joined in the chorus; some danced, others shouted, and all shook off the gloomy horrors of Van Diemen's Land.*

The Patriot and Hunter convicts, despite the hard labor, appear to have been slightly better treated than the regular convicts. According to Heustis, he asked that they, as political prisoners, be housed separately from the common criminals, and their custodians granted that request.

There is no record of any "political prisoner" being flogged, which was a common punishment for minor infractions. Stephen Wright recalled an

Ruins of the penitentiary in old Port Arthur, Tasmania. *Photo by the author.*

142

English prisoner tied to a wooden triangle for support and given seventy-five lashes with a cat-o-nine-tails for stealing a piece of beef:

> *There he was, strung upon a triangle. After the first blow, shreds of skin and flesh were flayed of by every one that followed: no groan or cry was uttered, but his face looked the perfect picture of agony. A surgeon was by, and occasionally felt his pulse, making him bear to the very highest degree all the torture that the system could stand without destroying his life. And when the bloody deed was finished, a pail of brine was dashed over his torn and quivering back, and yells of horror and pain broke from his ashy lips.*

> In their memoirs, Heustis, Marsh, Snow and Wright decried the near extermination of the Tasmanian natives because, as Snow and Marsh put it, "the English wanted their little island for a prison to enslave their poor white neighbors."

Miller wrote that ten floggings a day were common in the notorious Port Arthur and that many led to death, either then or in the hospital. But even there, Miller said fellow American Joseph Stewart was not flogged for an infraction that netted other men the agonizing lashes.

On his arrival home, James Gemmell wrote a letter, published widely in 1842, that described the horrors of the penal colony, including the statement: "I scarcely remember one American or Canadian who has not been flogged." Gemmell lied, probably to spur the American public to anger and the government to action.

TICKETS OF LEAVE GRANTED

Penal colony policy was to grant convicts a ticket of leave after a set period of hard work and good behavior. Normally, men sentenced to transport for life had to work eight years for a ticket of leave. But since the Patriots were not common criminals, Sir John Franklin granted an exception.

In March 1841, Sir John visited the main group of prisoners and stated that he had finally received an answer to his question about what to do with the American prisoners. The reply essentially was that the governor could indulge the prisoners in any fashion he chose other than allowing them to return home. Franklin then announced he would grant well-behaved men a ticket of leave once their period of labor equaled two years. To the men who arrived on the *Buffalo*, that meant ten more months of hard labor. For the Short Hills captives, the countdown to partial freedom was from five to nine months.

True to his word, the governor granted tickets of leave in August 1841 to the Short Hills prisoners from the *Marquis of Hastings*, including Wait and Chandler. After two years working on the road gangs, the governor granted prisoners from the *Canton* their tickets in January 1842 and those from the *Buffalo* theirs in February 1842. Some men had to wait longer, usually because of bad behavior.

The ticket allowed men to find paid employment within one of six districts in the interior of the island. The law forbade them access to coastal areas, fearing that they would escape aboard American whaling ships that frequented Tasmanian waters. Three prisoners convicted for their part in the Short Hills raid—Benjamin Wait, Samuel Chandler and James Gemmell—managed to escape that way and arrived home in 1842.

As Samuel Snow reported, a ticket of leave did not mean freedom:

> *We were sent out into the country immediately, and soon found that a ticket of leave was a Magna Charta on a very small scale; and that we held our liberty by a very precarious tenure; for, upon the slightest provocation, the almighty little country magistrate would wrest it from us.*

Once free to work, almost every man tried to earn money for a passage home in anticipation of an eventual pardon. That was difficult. A severe economic depression weighed on the island economy. Most available employment was on farms and seasonal in nature. Too many men competed for too few jobs, which drove wages down. Snow noted in his book that employers favored the Patriots over the regular convicts because of their honesty and good behavior.

The ticket-of-leave men no longer qualified for even the meager convict housing and rations. With work scarce, men struggled to survive. In one period just prior to leaving, Robert Marsh was without work and money for four months. He slept in the bush and ate mostly opossum and kangaroo.

Bad behavior lengthened the time to wait for a ticket of leave and could bring extra punishment. The worst penalty in the penal system, short of execution, was a term in the rough prison town at Port Arthur on the southeast corner of the island. The work conditions were reputed to be the harshest, and Port Arthur had a high death rate among its inmates.

Guard towers and the wall protecting the barracks in old Port Arthur. *Photo by the author.*

Horace Cooley and three other exiled Patriots—Michael Morin, William Reynolds and Jacob Paddock—escaped from Sandy Bay Probation Station after being on the island for just four months. Search parties found them three weeks later suffering from severe hunger. As punishment, the convict superintendent sent them to Port Arthur for two years.

Linus Miller and Joseph Stewart also failed at an escape attempt in 1840 and learned the horrors of Port Arthur. After a few months of hard labor at Port Arthur, Miller wrote that he was weak and not long for life. His status as an educated man saved him. A senior officer hired him as a tutor for his children. Stewart lucked into a paid job as a signalman. When Sir John Franklin left his post for England in 1843, Miller and Stewart applied for and received tickets of leave and left Port Arthur.

GRAND ESCAPES FROM VAN DIEMEN'S LAND

Of the many attempts to escape the penal island by the Patriot and Hunter prisoners, three men succeeded: Benjamin Wait, Samuel Chandler and James Gemmell.

Samuel Chandler, circa 1850. *Western University Archives.*

In August 1841, after two years working on a ranch, Wait and Chandler received their tickets of leave. Chandler used his new freedom to plan their escape. A Mason, he located lodge brothers in Hobart Town who helped arrange clandestine passage on an American whaling ship.

Just after Christmas 1841, Chandler and Wait obtained passes from their employer (rewards for good work) and traveled to Hobart Town. They rented a rowboat on the pretext of fishing and rowed out to sea. They spent three days in anxious uncertainty until their escape ship located them.

On the journey home, Wait and Chandler helped hunt whales and survived a shipwreck off South America. In Rio de Janeiro, another American captain agreed to take them to New York. They arrived in July 1842. Masons paid their train fare to Niagara Falls, New York, where they reunited with their families.

On January 27, 1842, James Gemmell received his ticket of leave and began planning his escape. He needed to shed his convict clothing first. He walked from the interior to Hobart Town and asked the superintendent of convicts for his original clothes to be returned from storage. Instead of clothes, guards handcuffed Gemmell for being outside of his allowed area and marched him from town with several other convicts. At lunch, a constable removed Gemmell's handcuffs to let him eat. Gemmell seized his musket and disappeared.

Gemmell's predicament was severe. If caught, he'd lose his ticket of leave and might be sent to Port Arthur. He had to escape. That night, he crept into Hobart Town and told a group of American sailors his story and troubles. They agreed to take him on board their whaler without the captain's knowledge. Gemmell's new friends hid him in the ship's hold under old sails and tarps.

A great risk remained. Harbor police thoroughly searched every ship leaving the harbor. Constables boarded looking for escapees. They poked their bayonets between the cargo in the hold. One blade pierced Gemmell's leg above the knee, he wrote. He did not cry out. Later, his new friends bound the wound and brought him food and clothing. He worked for his passage home.

Though he escaped a month after Wait and Chandler, he arrived home one month sooner, on June 22, 1842.

Following these successful escapes, the penal authorities tightened restrictions on access to the coasts for all convicts.

Pardons Granted, Men Sail Home

In 1843, the penal government conscripted forty American ticket-of-leave men to help hunt a notorious gang of bushrangers (escaped convicts who robbed and murdered). Two veterans of the Battle of the Windmill, Stephen Wright and Aaron Dresser, aided in the successful apprehension of the gang. As a reward, the British government granted them pardons and paid their way home. They embarked for England on July 2, 1843. As soon as they returned to New York State, they jointly published a letter in an attempt to shame the American government into helping their comrades. They described the rough state of other Patriot prisoners and their horrific living conditions,

On October 12, 1844, twenty-nine men, including Samuel Snow, Robert Marsh, Linus Miller and Daniel Heustis, received their free pardons. Over the next several years, surviving Patriot or Hunter prisoners received pardons, with a few exceptions. A pardon meant they could leave the island, but no man had saved enough money to buy passage home. They became economic prisoners.

U.S. diplomat Edward Everett, the ambassador to England, lobbied long and hard for pardons. His efforts paid off. Other than his diplomatic efforts, the American government abandoned its citizens in Van Diemen's Land. It provided no cash or ships to get the men home. Upper Canada had no interest in the wellbeing of its transported citizens. The Americans and Canadians were on their own.

For some of the pardoned, their chance to leave came in January 1845. The *Steiglitz*, an American whaler in the command of Captain Selah Young, came to Hobart Town for minor repairs. Heustis and others quickly made the captain's acquaintance and explained their predicament. Captain Young agreed to take some men on as replacement crew (he abandoned fourteen of his crew in Hobart Town for bad behavior, according to Snow), and he accepted the word of others that he would be paid once the passengers arrived back in America.

Young explained that the ship was bound for the northwest coast of America looking for whales, but he promised that if he should fall in with a ship homeward bound, he would get them aboard or leave them on an island in the Pacific Ocean on a main shipping route.

On January 29, 1845, the ship departed Tasmania with over two dozen men, including Heustis, Marsh and Snow. (The number varies from twenty-five to twenty-seven, depending on the author.) The *Steiglitz* stopped in Honolulu, where all but seven of the former prisoners got off. Groups of men made their own arrangements to get home from Hawaii. Heustis carried on to California and arrived in New York on June 15, 1846. Marsh landed on the east coast on March 9, 1846, while Snow arrived on May 2, 1846.

Miller used borrowed money to buy passage on a merchant ship and departed for home on September 25, 1845. He arrived in Philadelphia on January 27, 1846.

Sad Tale of Elijah Woodman

Like most rebel prisoners, Elijah Woodman earned his ticket of leave after two years' hard labor in Van Diemen's Land. Granted a pardon on July 23, 1845, he had no way to return home—ships and passage money were both scarce. By then almost forty-eight, he suffered from tuberculosis and the affects of hard work as a convict laborer. In addition, he had an eye ailment that took most of his sight. Destitute, he often relied on the generosity of fellow prisoners, such as James Aitchison, and the Hobart Town Masonic Lodge for food and clothing.

Woodman finally arranged for a berth on an American whaler, setting sail on the *Young Eagle* on March 1, 1847. His health continued to deteriorate. He died on June 13 at age fifty and was buried at sea on June 15. Fellow passenger Henry Shew, a carpenter and former Hunter captured at the Battle of the Windmill, built a coffin for Woodman.

Throughout his ordeal in the antipodes, Woodman had corresponded with his family in London, Upper Canada. He also kept a journal. In his

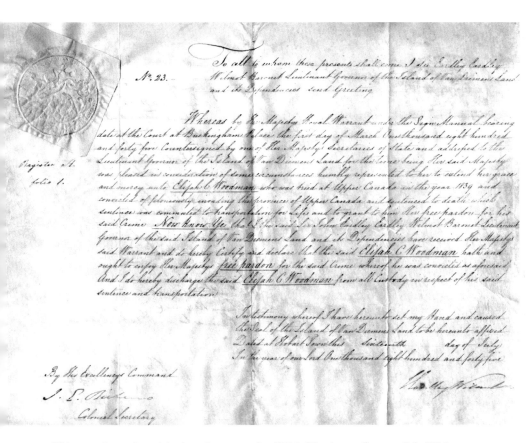

This scan shows the original pardon granted to Elijah Woodman. *Courtesy of the Elijah Woodman Family fonds, Western Archives, Western University.*

last days on the *Young Eagle*, too weak to write, he dictated journal entries to a ship's officer.

A few days after his burial, the whaler sank at sea. The officer managed to save Woodman's journal and eventually returned it to his heirs. Woodman's family passed the letters and journal down through generations.

Of the many published personal accounts by Patriot War rebels, the biography of Elijah Crocker Woodman appeared last, 113 years after his death. In 1960, author Fred Landon released *An Exile from Canada to Van Diemen's Land*, based on Woodman's own words. The source material now resides at the Western University in London, Ontario.

JOHN BERRY: LAST MAN HOME

Before the Patriot War, John Berry farmed near the present-day city of Brockville, Ontario. As he was an ardent reformer, the paranoid Upper Canada government arrested him on flimsy charges in the days following the Mackenzie rebellion. Once released, Berry moved to New York State and joined other Canadian refugees in the Hunters Lodge.

At age forty, John Berry was older than most men who participated in the Battle of the Windmill. Captured, tried and convicted, he sailed on the *Buffalo* to Van Diemen's Land with the other prisoners.

After receiving his ticket of leave, Berry worked as a shepherd in a remote district of the island. Pardoned in 1844, Berry remained ignorant of that fact until 1857. Upon hearing of his freedom, Berry arranged working passage on a whaling ship. After several years at sea, he arrived at New York in 1860.

Berry traveled across the state to Cape Vincent and took passage on a steamer headed to Brockville. On board, former Upper Canada Solicitor General William Draper recognized Berry as one of the prisoners he had prosecuted in 1839 after the windmill battle. Draper apparently shook Berry's hand and wished him well. Berry arrived at Brockville twenty-two years after he departed at age sixty-one—the last known transportee to come home.

THOSE WHO STAYED BEHIND

Historical records show that thirteen of the original ninety-two Patriot and Hunter transportees died far from home. Once pardoned, not all surviving Hunter and Patriot prisoners could or would go home.

For thirty-three survivors, there is no clear record that they ever returned. Not all of them disappeared without a trace, as this section relates. Several remained in Van Diemen's Land or settled on the Australian mainland. For any young man, especially a skilled worker from America's pioneer communities, Australia's growing economy offered opportunities. And in the 1850s, the biggest gold rush in modern history swept though the southeast corner of Australia.

James Milne Aitchison, originally from a wealthy family in Scotland, came to Canada in 1834. After some poor business deals and a stint at forgery (partly caused by heavy alcohol consumption), he fled to America in 1838.

Swept up in the Patriot movement, he joined the Battle of Windsor, was captured and transported. After his pardon in December 1844, he remained in Hobart Town, working odd jobs and doing what he could to assist the ailing Elijah Woodman. In late 1846 or early 1847, he traveled to Australia. There is no record that Aitchison, by then outcast from his Scottish family, ever left that continent.

Jacob Beemer, his father Joseph and his uncle David all played roles in the Duncombe uprising in 1837. When it failed, Jacob surrendered but was soon released. Later, when he discovered that he was to be indicted, he absconded to America and joined the Patriots. The British transported him for his part in the Short Hills raid. The books by Linus Miller and Benjamin Wait both called Jacob a traitor for snitching on his comrades, though their evidence is scanty. He remained in Van Diemen's Land after his pardon in July 1848. That year, at age thirty-four, he married Ann Walker (despite having a wife in Canada). They had three children. Records suggest that Beemer journeyed to Australia, got in trouble and returned to Van Diemen's Land again in chains for another period. After his first wife died, Beemer married a second time and sired two more children. He never went home.

Chauncey Bugby, an American from New York State transported after his capture at the Battle of the Windmill, married Elizabeth Hughes in Hobart Town in July 1846. Chauncey remained in VDL for life.

American George B. Cooley was transported for his part in the Short Hills raid. While most of his fellow Patriot inmates received pardons, his name remained off the list. Historian Cassandra Pybus speculates that the American consul who drafted the pardon list confused George with Horace Cooley. Frustrated, George attempted to escape the island in 1846. Upon his capture, he lost his ticket of leave and found himself again sentenced to hard labor. Finally pardoned in 1852, he moved to Australia.

Horace Cooley was transported for his role in a raid near the St. Clair River. Though issued a pardon in 1844, he waited until 1849 for freedom because the pardon had not been gazetted (published). Records suggest that Cooley never left Van Diemen's Land. A biography of common convict Henry Woods mentions that Woods was a tenant in a residence on the island in 1859 owned by a former convict named Horace Cooley.

Moses A. Dutcher, an American from New York State transported after his capture at the Battle of the Windmill, married Sarah Burchall in Van Diemen's Land and sired a daughter, Sarah Louisa, all before September 1844. That date implies that he married before his pardon arrived. The couple had one more daughter and then moved to Hawaii in 1849. Moses died in Honolulu about 1855 at age forty.

Ira Polly (or Polley), an American from New York State transported after his capture at the Battle of the Windmill, left Van Diemen's Land on the same whaler as Marsh, Snow and Heustis. After a stop in Hawaii, he changed direction and sailed to Australia. He became a farmer and family man in New South Wales. He died on January 1, 1898, age about seventy-one.

William Reynolds, an American from New York State transported after his capture at the Battle of the Windmill, also did not make the pardon list. Cassandra Pybus speculates that his was another case of name confusion. A man arrested at Short Hills, whose true name was David Deal, used William Reynolds as an alias. Deal/Reynolds had been transported but was pardoned during a stopover in England. The real William Reynolds escaped the island in 1850, but there is no record of him having come home.

Hiram Sharp, an American from New York State, was transported for his part in the Battle of the Windmill. Pardoned in October 1844, he left the island on an American whaling vessel, the *Belle*, for a voyage in the South Seas in August 1845. Some years later, he disembarked in Sydney. He stayed in Australia and married Mary Ann Black, a widow with four children, in 1850. They had five more children. Sharp died in 1859 at about forty-six.

Joseph Stewart, another American from New York State transported after his capture at the Battle of the Windmill, was pardoned in 1844, but it was not gazetted. He escaped the island in 1850, likely with William Reynolds. There is no record of him having come home.

Samuel Washburn, an American from New York State transported for his part in the Battle of the Windmill, married a transported convict, Agnes Scott, in Hobart Town in 1846. A year later, they moved to Australia.

Conclusion

The campaign to "liberate" Upper Canada failed for several reasons. The Patriot and Hunter leaders assumed the democratically deprived Canadians would flock to their rebel banner as soon as they showed force of arms in the colony. That was their greatest blunder. The majority of colonial residents stayed loyal to the queen, even when they disliked her colonial administrators. The invaders did not have the training, the officers, the supplies or the logistics to succeed on their own without widespread support from Canadians.

There was also a failure on the part of a majority of Patriots and Hunters to deliver on their promises. In his memoirs published in 1848, Robert Marsh attests to this: "The failure of the Patriots in the years 1837–1838… was not so much the fault of those who actually took up arms and done as they had agreed, as it was of those who failed to fulfill their promises."

The lives lost and ruined in the Patriot War may seem to have been in vain. There was no clear victory as in the Texas Revolution. For any Canadian or American who fought for freedom in 1837 and 1838, they can be forgiven for thinking it a wasted effort. But they did make a difference. Change did come on the heels of the Upper and Lower Canada rebellions. Britain's colonial masters had snubbed delegations and ignored negative reports on the dysfunctional, self-serving colonial governments for years. The two colonial rebellions in Canada and the fortune (the pounds equivalent was $10 million) Britain spent fighting Patriot and Hunter invasions for a year woke up the lounging lion. Sensing that something must be amiss as early as mid-1838, England appointed a new governor general for Canada, Lord Durham.

To his political opponents, John George Lambton, forty-six, the Earl of Durham, was known as "Radical Jack." He created a storm of protest from the Canadian elite when he submitted his report on Upper and Lower Canada to the Colonial Office on February 4, 1839. The report confirmed that the two colonial governments consisted of corrupt, nepotistic and elitist cliques.

Lambton made two main democratic recommendations: replace the executive councils with a cabinet composed of elected members, and unite Upper and Lower Canada.

The British government of the day balked at abolishing the existing appointed executive councils. It took a change in England's ruling party in 1847 before responsible government came to the Canadian colonies.

Britain did move quickly on the second part. In 1840, it created a single colony called the United Province of Canada, or simply Canada, with the first election held in 1841. Though one colony in name, a political distinction between Canada West (Ontario) and Canada East (Quebec) remained.

Another recommendation from Durham, which England did enact, was to sell all land set aside during colonization for the Church of England, since the colony had not granted land to other denominations. The selling of these clergy reserves by the Family Compact and the misused income from such sales had helped incite the rebellion.

One paragraph in Lord Durham's report won the hearts of Canadian rebellion refugees and their American friends by confirming what they knew to be true:

> *It certainly appeared too much as if the rebellion had been purposely invited by the Government, and the unfortunate men who took part in it deliberately drawn into a trap by those who subsequently inflicted so severe a punishment on them for their error. It seemed, too, as if the dominant party made use of the occasion afforded it by the real guilt of a few desperate and imprudent men in order to persecute or disable the whole body of their political opponents. A great number of perfectly innocent individuals were thrown into prison and suffered in person, property and character. The whole body of reformers was subjected to suspicion, and to harassing proceedings instituted by magistrates whose political leanings were notoriously averse to them. Severe laws were passed under color of which individuals very generally esteemed were punished without any form of trial.*

The Durham report, combined with a backlash against the injustices of the Family Compact, allowed the political reform movement to take control of the government. The reformers granted pardons to all rebels and rebel leaders between 1843 and 1849.

> While a storm of public opinion raged over his report, Lord Durham died of tuberculosis July 28, 1840.

The changes brought about by Lord Durham gave Marsh some consolation, as he noted in the closing pages of his memoirs:

> *I am of the opinion of many whom I have conversed with in Canada: that it could not be a bad cause, when it has been the means of bringing about so much good to the people of Canada; and although many have not lived to see it, and others have suffered much in bringing it about, the good results will be distilled in the minds of the rising generation.*

In his biography, William Gates recalls a conversation with a man from Kingston shortly after Gates returned from the penal colony:

> *He said that Canada had been greatly benefitted by the outbreak in which we had been concerned; and although it had failed, and he had cruelly suffered therefore, they had secured nearly all the privileges at first desired.*

John Charles Dent, in his 1885 history of the Upper Canada rebellion, conceded that the unrest brought tangible benefits:

> *It aroused public opinion in England to the reality of Canadian grievances. It proclaimed aloud to the nation that the cherished colonial system—so far, at any rate, as Canada was concerned—had survived its usefulness; that the perennial complaints of Canadian Reformers had not been the mere inventions of an angry and jealous-minded Opposition; that a large part of the population of Canada had for years groaned under abuses such as no people worthy to enjoy the blessings of freedom could be expected to endure with patience; and that they would no longer quietly submit to be treated like the children of a professedly beneficent, but in reality cold, indifferent, and unsympathizing parent.*

It is the nature of Canadian politics that change comes slowly through negotiation and compromise, not revolution. The Patriot War did not win freedom immediately, but it made the political masters fix a problem they had too long ignored and far sooner than would have occurred otherwise. The Patriot War forced a change in governance in favor of democratic institutions. That renewed political culture created fertile ground for the creation of an independent Canada in 1867.

What Happened To...

After the Patriot War, the survivors and those who came home from Van Diemen's Land went on with their lives, where Fate bestowed honors, ignominy, prosperity, penury, fame or obscurity.

ROBERT ALWAY (1790–August 6, 1840). Born in Gloucester, England, Alway arrived in Upper Canada around 1816 and became a farmer. He ran for office in 1834 and was elected to the Upper Canada assembly as a reformer. The colony placed a £250 reward for his capture after the Duncombe uprising for encouraging the unrest. Arrested, the courts released him for insufficient evidence. Shortly after, he left the colony for Texas, where he died of yellow fever.

GILMAN APPLEBY (August 29, 1806–February 18, 1867). After the Patriot War, Gilman became prosperous through land sales and ship ownership. He built the steamer *Sultana* and launched it in the spring of 1847 as the captain. That ship served as a floating extension of the Underground Railway. No escaped slave was ever turned away and was ensured passage to safety in Canada. But Gilman had his dark side. In July 1839, while sailing the *Constitution* from Detroit to Buffalo, he lured fifteen-year-old Miss Westfall to his stateroom and sexually assaulted her. Gilman was arrested and committed to trial. Due to family shame and public notoriety, the young lady never appeared to give evidence in court. Gilman's only conviction came in the court of public opinion.

SIR GEORGE ARTHUR (June 21, 1784–September 19, 1854). Arthur left Upper Canada for England in 1841 and was made a baronet as a reward. (He'd already been knighted for his service in Van Diemen's Land.) In 1842, the government posted him to India as governor of Bombay. Later, England promoted him to major general and made him a member of the Privy Council.

WILLIAM LEWIS BABY (April 13, 1812–November 9, 1897). William was born in Sandwich, Upper Canada, a son of colonial leader James (Jacques) Baby. He had three wives and at least two children in his long life. He received a patronage appointment as the customs officer at Windsor on October 30, 1873, which continued to 1882. He wrote his memoirs in 1896.

LUCIUS VERUS BIERCE (August 4, 1801–November 11, 1870). After resigning as the Hunters Lodge army commander, Bierce returned to his legal career. Beginning in 1839, he won the first of five non-consecutive terms as Akron mayor. He won one term as Ohio state senator. He married for a second time in 1840 (his first wife and son died in 1839) and had one daughter. He served as president of the board of education and as a Grand Master of the Ohio Masons in 1853. Though in his sixties, he joined the Union army in 1863 as a major and served two years as assistant adjutant general of the Ohio Volunteers. In 1873, he helped found the Bierce Library at Buchtel College, now part of the University of Akron. He donated much of his personal collection—likely including the sword he took from Dr. Hume—much of which was destroyed by fire in 1899.

EDWIN D. BRADLEY (August 28, 1804–November 1, 1890). At the start of the Mexican-American War in 1846, Bradley raised a company of volunteers and served as their captain under General Zachary Taylor. After that war, Bradley worked as a mercantile trader in Ohio. At the outbreak of the Civil War, Bradley recruited another volunteer company. He rose to the rank of colonel and commanded the Thirty-eighth Ohio Volunteer Regiment. He married Eliza Guinall, twenty-one, in 1843 and had three sons, one who also fought in the Civil War. He married Kate Abbott, thirty-three, in 1857.

JAMES DOUGALL (September 21, 1810–April 5, 1888). After the Patriot War, Dougall moved to Amherstburg and became an agent for a different bank and a gentleman farmer. He went through periods of business prosperity and failure. He moved back to Windsor and became the first mayor of the village after its incorporation. He served on various boards and commissions. After his first wife died, he remarried and had two more daughters.

CHARLES DROLET (May 8, 1795–September 22, 1873). Following the escape of Dr. Edward Theller with his help, Charles Drolet fled to America just ahead of an arrest warrant. He practiced law in Buffalo and Detroit until the general amnesty in 1849. Back in Lower Canada, he received two patronage appointments: clerk of the Court of Vice-Admiralty in 1850, and later, deputy clerk of the Court of Appeal. He held both positions until his death.

DR. CHARLES DUNCOMBE (July 28, 1792–October 1, 1867). After the Patriot cause collapsed, Dr. Duncombe stayed in the northern states, lecturing and practicing medicine. Though pardoned in 1843, he never returned to Canada other than to briefly visit old friends. He settled in Sacramento in 1849 and served terms in the California legislature. He died of complications from sunstroke.

SIR JOHN FRANKLIN (April 16, 1786–June 11, 1847). Franklin left Van Diemen's Land in 1843 to return to England. Four years later, he met his destiny in the Canadian Arctic.

WILLIAM GATES (1814–1865?). Pardoned in September 1845, Gates went to Australia, where he labored on sheep ranches for two years to earn his fare home. Arriving in America on May 31, 1848, he traveled overland to the family home in Cape Vincent. His parents had moved, his eldest brother had died and his siblings had scattered. He located his parents in the Canadian village of Aylmer, south of London. He paid them a visit and convinced them to return to America. They settled in Wilson, New York. In 1850, Gates published his memoirs.

JAMES GEMMELL (February 4, 1814–April 6, 1881). After his return, Gemmell moved to Michigan and married. After the death of his wife and son, he moved to Utah and became a Mormon. He had a score of children from several wives. The Mormons excommunicated him in November 1858. He moved with one wife and their family to Montana in 1859. He spent the rest of his life there, trading with Indians and operating a sawmill.

HENRY S. HANDY (1804–1846). Henry Handy faded from the public mind as interest in the Patriot cause dissipated. He died relatively young in Bayfield, Michigan.

JOHN H. HARMON (June 21, 1819–August 6, 1888). Born in Portage County, Ohio, Harmon learned the printer's trade at his father's newspaper in Ravenna, Ohio. In 1838, he traveled to Detroit as the aide-de-camp of General Lucius V. Bierce and followed him into war. After the Battle of Windsor, Harmon took a job at the *Detroit Free Press*, eventually becoming part owner by 1841. That year, he married Sarah S. Rood. They had three children. Harmon become sole owner of the newspaper by 1853 and then sold it the following year. Harmon served as a city alderman in 1847 and as mayor in 1852 and 1853. He served as customs collector for the Port of Detroit from 1854 to 1857.

JOSIAH HENSON (June 15, 1789–May 5, 1883). In 1842, Henson founded a settlement for fugitive slaves at Dawn Township (near present-day Dresden, Ontario). The facility prospered, with about five hundred residents at its peak, and included farms, a gristmill, a sawmill and a brickyard. They exported black walnut lumber and furniture to the United States and Britain. Henson inspired the title character of Harriet Beecher Stowe's novel *Uncle Tom's Cabin* and is the first black man to have his portrait on a Canadian stamp. Matthew Henson, Josiah's great-grand nephew, accompanied Admiral Robert Peary to the North Pole in 1909.

DANIEL DUNBAR HEUSTIS (April 8, 1806–1853). Heustis gave up a comfortable life as a Watertown, New York merchant to join the Patriots in January 1838. He participated in two raids, the second being the Battle of the Windmill. On returning from exile, he learned that his first wife had divorced him to remarry. He married Mary Starkey on November 19, 1847. The couple, with Daniel's mother, Abigail, moved to Wayne County, Michigan, where Daniel worked as a police officer. They had a daughter. According to family records, he died in 1853 during one of the periodic cholera outbreaks, an ironic ending for a man who had survived the filth and pestilence of prison ships and slavery.

JEDEDIAH HUNT JR. (1815–1860). Following the Patriot War, Jedediah settled in the village of Chilo, Ohio. He married Jane Ann Scott, and together they had six children. He held the position of Chilo postmaster from 1846 to

1851 and from 1855 to 1860. He wrote articles for a variety of magazines and published newspapers. He became an accomplished poet who famously tangled with Edgar Allan Poe in critical newspaper articles.

BENJAMIN LETT (November 14, 1813–December 9, 1858). After his arrest for numerous crimes in New York 1841, Lett fell ill in the harsh prison conditions. His devoted brother, Thomas (June 17, 1809–July 8, 1885), worked hard for his brother's early release. Governor Silas Wright pardoned Lett on March 10, 1845. Benjamin moved to the family farm and left his terrorist life behind. He died under mysterious circumstances in Milwaukee. Thomas claimed that agents of the Canadian government had lured him away and poisoned him with strychnine.

WILLIAM LYON MACKENZIE (March 12, 1795–August 28, 1861). Relegated to the sidelines (or preferring to be there) during the rebellion, Mackenzie continued publishing his polemics when his funds allowed. He spent eleven months in prison (1839–40) for breaking the United States neutrality law. Mackenzie ultimately came to regret his involvement in the Patriot War and wrote that he was glad it failed. While living in the United States, the brutality of slavery and the rapaciousness of the nineteenth-century corporate monopolies soured him on American republicanism. After his pardon in February 1849, he returned to Toronto and spent another seven years (1851–58) as a member of the colonial legislature. Though the Family Compact was gone and many reforms enacted, he never stopped demanding equality for all and an end to favoritism. His grandson, William Lyon Mackenzie King, served as Canada's tenth and longest-sitting prime minister.

COLONEL ALLAN NAPIER MACNAB (February 19, 1798–August 8, 1862). The Patriot War gave a great boost to Allan MacNab's career, propelling him from the provincial backwater of Hamilton to the center of colonial politics. His order to burn the *Caroline* gained him a knighthood in 1838, even though it likely prolonged hostilities. After the war, Sir Allan struggled to retain the old Tory ways against a rising tide of reform politics. Time and pragmatism moderated his temper enough that he became premier of Canada West (now Ontario) between 1854 and 1856.

ELIAKIM MALCOLM (March 18, 1801 September 26, 1874). Upon his return to Upper Canada, Eliakim continued in business as a farmer and miller.

Drawn to local politics, he became the first reeve of Oakland Township in 1850 after its formation and the first warden of Brant County in 1853 when it separated from a larger county. He and his wife, Samantha, had eight children.

PIERRE MARENTETTE (March 19, 1799–February 8, 1872). Marentette was born into the large French Canadian community in southwestern Upper Canada. He married Archange Groulx, seventeen, on June 14, 1825. They had twelve children together. A blacksmith by trade, one of his roles was to shackle prisoners in the local jail. Marentette was active in the local militia and became a lieutenant in the Second Essex militia regiment on September 23, 1838. He participated in the orchard fight at the Battle of Windsor. He was appointed a militia captain on August 25, 1848. Grateful townsfolk elected him a member of the first Sandwich town council in 1858.

ROBERT MARSH (1812–1880?). Marsh participated in three raids into Upper Canada during the Patriot War, including the first and the last. In his memoirs, published in 1848, he demonstrated an unflinching belief in American-style democracy and an unbending dislike of British colonial rule. Despite seven years of hard times, his closing chapter summed up his belief that he had fought the good fight. Following the book's publication, Marsh dropped out of the historical record. U.S. census data shows that he worked as a laborer and did not marry. The 1870 and 1880 censuses list Robert as living in the household of his sister Mary (married to William Moore) in Erie, Pennsylvania.

DONALD MCLEOD (January 1, 1779–July 22, 1879). Britain pardoned McLeod in 1846. He returned to Canada and took a federal government job. After retirement, he moved to Cleveland, Ohio, where he remained until dying at age 101.

LINUS WILSON MILLER (December 28, 1817–April 11, 1880). Miller returned from Van Diemen's Land to Stockton, New York, to find his parents and siblings alive and well. Miller, still a young man, picked up the threads of his life. He wrote his memoirs and became a farmer and dairyman. In January 1850, he married Anne Jeanette Curtis. They had two sons and three daughters.

ELIAS MOORE (March 1, 1776–October 13, 1847). After the American Revolution, the Moore family fled "the persecution Quakers suffered for their neutral stand during the American Revolution" and settled initially in Nova Scotia. Elias moved to the Norwich area of Upper Canada in 1818. In 1834, Moore won one of the seats in the Middlesex riding for the reformers, becoming one of the first Quakers elected in Canada. Moore participated in the growing pre-rebellion tension in 1837. He was arrested for treason but was never tried. He retained his seat in the assembly until February 1840. Moore served as clergy reserve inspector until his death, helping to implement Lord Durham's recommendation to sell the clergy lands.

JOHN PRINCE (March 12, 1796–November 30, 1870). Following the Patriot War, Prince was elected to the assembly of the newly named colony Canada West in 1841. He was repeatedly reelected until stepping down in 1854. In February 1849, the always hot-tempered Prince met the newly pardoned William Lyon Mackenzie in the parliamentary library in Montreal. The colonel threatened to kick Mackenzie down the stairs if he did not leave immediately. The diminutive Mackenzie complied. Prince began advocating for Canada's independence from England as early as 1850. He served in the assembly again from 1857 to 1860, after which he accepted an appointment as a judge. During the Fenian raids in 1866, he offered his military services and threatened to execute any captured prisoners.

ELIJAH JACKSON ROBERTS (1802–April 26, 1851). After the Patriot War, Roberts served his community and state with distinction. His roles included: member of the first Detroit Board of Education organized March 15, 1842, and its first school inspector; clerk of the Michigan House of Representatives in 1839 and from 1841 to 1843; adjutant general of Michigan from 1842 to 1844, and state senator from the Sixth District in 1851.

HENRY SHERWOOD (1807–July 7, 1855). Sherwood profited politically from his tough handling of the Battle of Windsor prisoners. He served as the seventh mayor of Toronto from 1842 to 1844, as solicitor general of Canada West in 1842 and as the fourth premier of Canada West from May 28, 1847, to March 11, 1848. He died from illness while vacationing in Bavaria.

ABRAM DANIEL SMITH (June 9, 1811–June 4, 1865). Following the failure of the Hunters, Smith moved to Milwaukee, Wisconsin. After unsuccessful attempts to enter politics, Smith formed a law firm and was later elected to the state Supreme Court, a position he held from 1853 to 1859. In 1854, he presided over a case that struck a blow against slavery. Federal marshals arrested an escaped slave living in Wisconsin, Joshua Glover, under the U.S. Fugitive Slave Act. They intended to return him to his master. Abolitionist Sherman Booth broke Glover from jail and spirited him away. Booth was arrested for aiding a fugitive slave. The case came before Smith, who eventually ruled that the fugitive act was unconstitutional. It remained that way in Wisconsin, even after Smith's judgment was overturned by the U.S. Supreme Court. Smith died under mysterious circumstances after the Civil War while returning home from a stint in South Carolina as a federally appointed tax commissioner.

Samuel D. Snow (1800–1867?). Born in Massachusetts, Snow settled in Cuyahoga County, Ohio, as an adult. On returning from exile to Ohio, he found his wife, Mary, and four children well. He wrote his brief memoirs of his Patriot army service that same year. In 1850, Samuel and Mary (they were fifty and forty-six, respectively) had their fifth and last child. Snow's son Edwin died fighting in the Civil War in 1862. He lost an older daughter in 1861 and his wife in 1863. Public records show him alive in 1866, but he does not appear in the 1870 census.

Thomas Jefferson Sutherland (1801–September 7, 1852). For a time after the Patriot War, Sutherland turned his energies to writing pamphlets and books. Between 1839 and 1841, he published a book of prose and poetry called *Loose Leaves*; a pamphlet calling for the president to release Mackenzie from prison; *Letter to Lord Brougham*, in which he pleaded for the release of American prisoners in Van Diemen's Land; and a collection of letters to Queen Victoria, Lord Durham and Sir George Arthur in which he urged the release of Americans held in the penal colony and described his legal efforts to obtain his release from confinement in the Quebec Citadel. By the 1850s, Sutherland was a drifter in the Midwest, making a living writing and lecturing on phrenology. On September 7, 1852, he died of typhus at the Iowa, Sac and Fox native mission in Highland, Kansas, and was buried there among other victims of disease.

Samuel A. "Squire" Thayer (1806–1879?). Born in Richmond, New Hampshire, Squire was a working-class guy (laborer, barrel maker, carpenter) who heeded the call to help liberate Canada. Following his release from the Citadel, Thayer enlisted in the U.S. Army but deserted in December 1839.

His army record described him as five feet, nine inches tall, with light blue eyes, dark hair and a fair complexion. He enlisted again for the Union in 1861, fought in Tennessee with the Illinois infantry and received a disability discharge a year later. In 1867, he married a twenty-nine-year-old widow with four children, Barthena, and sired a child with her in 1872. In the 1880 census, Barthena Thayer was listed as a widow.

DR. EDWARD ALEXANDER THELLER (January 13, 1804–February 7, 1859). Dr. Theller moved from Detroit to Rochester, New York, in 1841. While the Patriot War was over and the Hunters Lodge nearly defunct, he remained combative. He plotted with Benjamin Lett and others to blow up the Welland Canal. All the evidence points to Dr. Theller as being the actual bomber who destroyed one lock and the two schooners moored nearby on September 9, 1841. In 1841, his book *Canada in 1837–38* was published. A readable mixture of historical fact and propaganda, it rekindled hatred of the British along the border at a time when tensions had begun to cool. Dr. Theller remained an idealist for life and a supporter of the underdog. He strongly opposed slavery. He took his medical skills to Panama in 1849 to help victims of yellow fever. While there, he joined a rebellion that aimed to get independence from Colombia. A loser again, he fled to San Francisco in 1853. In 1856, he began a two-year stint as the superintendent of schools. Two years later, he moved to the gold fields near Hornitos, California, to practice medicine. He died there in 1859.

RENSSELAER VAN RENSSELAER (March 1802–January 1, 1850). Van Rensselaer spent six months in jail for his role in early raids on Canada. After his release, he married Euphemia "Mary" Foreman in November 1840. They had one child. He committed suicide by inhaling charcoal gas (carbon monoxide poisoning) on January 1, 1850.

BENJAMIN WAIT (September 7, 1813–November 9, 1895). Wait fought in three Patriot campaigns and was captured in a raid near Niagara in June 1838. After his escape from Van Diemen's Land, Wait published his memoirs in 1843 as a series of contrived letters between himself and his wife, Maria. Maria died in May 1843 after giving birth to twins. Wait remarried in 1845 and moved to Grand Rapids, Michigan. He became a lumberman and founded the *Northwestern Lumberman* magazine in 1873. He later lost his fortune and lived on charity for his final years.

Appendix I

Ross Wilkins (February 19, 1799–May 17, 1872). Born in Pittsburgh, Pennsylvania, Wilkins became a prosecutor by age twenty-one in that city. He was a member of the Pennsylvania House of Representatives from 1829 to 1830. President Andrew Jackson appointed him as a territorial judge in 1832 and then as a district judge for Michigan in 1836. He continued as a judge until his retirement in 1870.

Stephen Smith Wright (1813–1863). Five months after leaving Van Diemen's Land on a British brig, Stephen and Aaron Dresser arrived in England. Ambassador Edward Everett paid for the last leg of their voyage to New York. Wright spent two days in the company of William Lyon Mackenzie before going home to Denmark, New York. He published his memoirs in 1844.

Appendix II

Men Hanged and Transported

The biography of William Lyon Mackenzie by Charles Lindsey lists the names of 824 people arrested in Upper Canada between December 5, 1837, and November 1, 1838, for suspected treasonous activities or invasions of the colony. In addition, the colony captured and imprisoned 207 others after the windmill battle and the Windsor battle.

Of the 1,034 known arrestees in Upper Canada, the majority suffered no penalty other than a few weeks or months in a miserable jail. Two Patriot prisoners died of illness, probably pneumonia, while in custody. Anthony Van Egmond, sixty-two, who took part in Mackenzie's attack on Toronto, died on January 5, 1838. David Taylor, twenty-four, a captive in the Short Hills raid, died in Fort Henry on August 27, 1838.

This appendix lists the 112 prisoners who suffered the harshest legal penalties—execution or exile. The list includes raiders and rebels from both the western and eastern fronts of the Patriot War. It does not include men who escaped before their sentences could be carried out or those released in England on their way to a penal colony.

While not included in these lists, the British also hanged 12 men captured during the Lower Canada rebellion. Lower Canada also transported 58 men to Australia and jailed over 1,000 for periods from a few days to several years.

APPENDIX II

MEN HANGED

Twenty men died at public executions in London, Hamilton, Toronto or Kingston, Upper Canada. Below are their names, approximate age (if known), nationality, date and city of execution and the event for which they were convicted. For some men, nationality is uncertain because they lived in both Upper Canada and America. In these cases, their nationality at birth is provided.

Dorrephus Abbey, forty-seven, American, December 12, 1838, Kingston, windmill battle

Duncan Anderson, forty-eight, American, January 4, 1839, Kingston, windmill battle

Daniel Bedford, twenty-seven, Canadian, January 11, 1839, London, Windsor battle

Christopher Buckley, thirty, American, January 4, 1839, Kingston, windmill battle

Albert Clark, twenty-one, American, January 14, 1839, London, Windsor battle

Cornelius Cunningham, thirty-two, American-born, February 4, 1839, London, Windsor battle

Joshua Gwillen Doan, twenty-eight, Canadian, February 6, 1939, London, Windsor battle

Daniel George, twenty-seven, American, December 12, 1838, Kingston, windmill battle

Sylvester Lawton, twenty-eight, American, January 4, 1839, Kingston, windmill battle

Lyman Leach, forty, American, February 11, 1839, Kingston, windmill battle

Samuel Lount, forty-six, Canadian, April 12, 1838, Toronto, Mackenzie rebellion

Hiram Benjamin Lynn, twenty-six, American, January 7, 1839, London, Windsor battle

Peter Matthews, fifty-two, Canadian, April 12, 1838, Toronto, Mackenzie rebellion

James Morreau, thirty-two, American, July 30, 1838, Hamilton, Short Hills raid

Joel Peeler, forty-one, American, December 22, 1838, Kingston, windmill battle

Amos Perley, Canadian-born, February 6, 1839, London, Windsor battle

Russell Phelps, thirty-eight, American, January 4, 1839, Kingston, windmill battle

Sylvanus Swete, twenty-one, American, December 22, 1838, Kingston, windmill battle

Nils Sholtewskii von Schoultz, thirty-one, Finnish, December 8, 1838, Kingston, windmill battle

Martin Woodruff, forty, American, December 19, 1838, Kingston, windmill battle

MEN TRANSPORTED

Ninety-two men journeyed by ship to the penal colony at Van Diemen's Land (VDL). Below are their names (most common spelling), approximate age when transported (if known), nationality, the raid for which they were transported and if they returned home. Return dates are when they arrived in eastern North America. For many, their final fate is unknown.

James Milne Aitchison, twenty-eight, Scottish, Windsor battle, went to Australia

David Allen, thirty-seven, American, windmill battle, returned 1845

Thomas Baker, forty-seven, American, windmill battle, fate unknown

Henry Verrelon Barnum, twenty-five, Canadian, Windsor battle, returned 1846

Jacob Beemer, twenty-nine, Canadian, Short Hills raid, stayed in VDL

John Berry, forty, Canadian, windmill battle, returned 1860

Orlin Blodget, twenty-three, American, windmill battle, fate unknown

John Bradley, thirty, Irish, windmill battle, fate unknown

George T. Brown, twenty-two, American, windmill battle, returned 1846

Chauncey Bugby, twenty-two, American, windmill battle, stayed in VDL

Hugh Calhoun, thirty-five, Irish, windmill battle, fate unknown

Samuel Chandler, forty-eight, American-born, Short Hills raid, returned 1842

Robert G. Collins, thirty-two, American, windmill battle, fate unknown

George B. Cooley, twenty-one, American, Short Hills raid, went to Australia

Horace Cooley, American-born, Lake St. Clair, pardoned, stayed in VDL

John Cronkhite, twenty-nine, American, windmill battle, returned 1846

Lysander Curtis, thirty-five, American, windmill battle, died in VDL

Luther Darby, forty-eight, American, windmill battle, returned 1846

Leonard Delano, twenty-six, American, windmill battle, returned 1846

Aaron Dresser, twenty-four, American, windmill battle, returned 1844

Moses A. Dutcher, twenty-three, American, windmill battle, settled in Hawaii

Elon Fellows, twenty-three, American, windmill battle, returned 1846

James DeWitt Fero, twenty-five, Canadian, Windsor battle, returned 1846

Michael Fraer, twenty-three, American, windmill battle, fate unknown

Emanuel Garrison, twenty-six, American, windmill battle, returned 1846

William Gates, twenty-four, American, windmill battle, returned 1848

James Gemmell, twenty-three, Scottish-American, Short Hills raid, returned 1842

John Gilman, thirty-eight, American, windmill battle, returned 1846

Gideon A. Goodrich, forty-three, American, windmill battle, returned 1846

John Grant (aka Grantham), twenty-one, Canadian, Short Hills raid, returned 1846

Jerry Griggs, twenty-one, American, windmill battle, returned 1846

Nelson Griggs, twenty-eight, American, windmill battle, returned 1846

John Seymour Gutridge, thirty, American, Windsor battle, fate unknown

Daniel Dunbar Heustis, thirty-two, American, windmill battle, returned 1846

Garret Hicks, forty-five, American, windmill battle, returned 1846

David House (aka Howth), twenty-six, Dutch, windmill battle, returned 1846

James Ingles, twenty-eight, Scottish, windmill battle, fate unknown

Andrew Leeper, forty-four, American, windmill battle, died in VDL

Joseph Leforte, twenty-nine, Canadian, windmill battle, return date unclear

Daniel Liscum, forty, American, windmill battle, returned 1846

Hiram Loop, twenty-five, American, windmill battle, fate unknown

Norman Mallory, twenty-four, American, Short Hills raid, fate unknown

Robert Marsh, twenty-five, American, Windsor battle, returned 1846

Foster H. Martin, thirty-four, American, windmill battle, died in VDL

Jeheil H. Martin, thirty-one, American, windmill battle, returned 1846

Calvin Mathers, twenty-five, American, windmill battle, fate unknown

Chauncey Mathers, twenty-five, American, windmill battle, fate unknown

Alexander McLeod, twenty-four, Canadian, Short Hills raid, died in VDL

John James McNulty, Canadian, Short Hills raid, died in VDL

Linus Miller, twenty-one, American, Short Hills raid, returned 1846

Andrew Moore, twenty-six, American, windmill battle, fate unknown

Michael Morin (aka Murray), thirty-one, American, Windsor battle, returned 1847

John Morrisette, twenty, Canadian, windmill battle, returned 1845

William Nottage, thirty-eight, Canadian-born, Windsor battle, died in VDL

Alson Owen, twenty-seven, American, windmill battle, died in VDL

Jacob Paddock, eighteen, American, windmill battle, fate unknown

James Pierce, twenty-two, American, windmill battle, returned 1846

Ira Polly, twenty-two, American, windmill battle, settled in Australia

Asa Priest, forty-five, American, windmill battle, died at sea on route to VDL

Solomon Reynolds, thirty-three, American, windmill battle, fate unknown

William Reynolds, nineteen, American, windmill battle, escaped VDL 1850

Asa H. Richardson, twenty-four, American, windmill battle, fate unknown

Hiram Sharp, twenty-five, American, windmill battle, settled in Australia

Chauncey Sheldon, fifty-seven, American, Windsor battle, returned 1846

Henry Shew, twenty-eight, American, windmill battle, returned 1852

John Henry Simmons, twenty-three, American, Windsor battle, died in VDL

Orin W. Smith, thirty-two, American, windmill battle, returned 1846

Samuel Snow, thirty-eight, American, Windsor battle, returned 1846

John Sprague, twenty-three, American, Windsor battle, fate unknown

Elizur Stevens, twenty-seven, American, Windsor battle, returned 1846

Joseph W. Stewart, twenty-five, American, windmill battle, escaped VDL 1850

Riley M. Stewart, thirty-one, American, Windsor battle, fate unknown

Thomas Stockton, forty, American, windmill battle, died in VDL

John G. Swanburg (aka Swansbury), twenty-eight, American, windmill battle, returned 1846

Alvin B. Sweet, twenty-two, American, Windsor battle, returned 1846

John Thomas, twenty-six, American, windmill battle, returned 1846

Joseph Thompson, twenty-six, American, windmill battle, returned 1846

John Burwell Tyrrell, twenty-four, Canadian, Windsor battle, first man pardoned, returned 1843

Garret Van Camp, twenty-nine, American, Short Hills raid, died in VDL

John Vernon, twenty-one, Canadian, Short Hills raid, fate unknown

James Waggoner, thirty-three, Canadian, Short Hills raid, fate unknown

Benjamin Wait, twenty-four, Canadian, Short Hills raid, returned 1842

Samuel Washburn, twenty-three, American, windmill battle, settled in Australia

Patrick White, twenty-five, Irish, windmill battle, fate unknown

Nathan Whiting, forty-five, American, windmill battle, returned 1846

Riley Whitney, twenty-eight, American, windmill battle, returned 1848

James Peter Williams, twenty-four, American, Windsor battle, died in VDL

John C. Williams, thirty-eight, American, Windsor battle, fate unknown

Edward A. Wilson, twenty-seven, American, windmill battle, returned 1846

Bemis Woodbury, twenty-two, American, windmill battle, returned 1846

Elijah Crocker Woodman, forty-two, American-born, Windsor battle, died at sea on route home

Stephen Smith Wright, twenty-five, American, windmill battle, returned 1844

Bibliography

This bibliography comes in three sections. The first section lists firsthand accounts—journals, notes, letters and memoirs—of people who participated in the Patriot War. The second section lists works by observers who lived in the era and recorded events or interviewed participants. The third section consists of sources by later historians.

Firsthand Accounts

Baby, William Lewis. *Souvenirs of the Past*. Windsor, ON, 1896. Baby participated in the defense of western Upper Canada.

Bierce, Lucius Versus. *Historical Reminiscences of Summit County*. Akron, OH: T and N.G. Canfield, 1854. Bierce led the attack on Windsor.

Dewy, Francis A. *Michigan Pioneer Collections*. Vol. 7. Lansing, MI: Thorp & Godfrey, 1886. Contains personal accounts from Canadian defender James Dougall about the Battle of Windsor and from American raider Robert McFarlan about the Battle of Fighting Island published in the *Detroit Free Press* on March 1, 1885.

Gates, William. *Recollections of Life in Van Diemen's Land*. Lockport, NY: George Mackaness, 1850. Gates participated in the Battle of the Windmill.

Grant, Henry C. *Western Herald and Farmers' Magazine*. Sandwich, UC: July 3, 1838, page 6 (http://news2.ourontario.ca/2352157/page/6), and December 11, 1838, pages 4-5 (http://news2.ourontario.ca/2352179/page/4). Grant participated in the defense of western Upper Canada.

Henson, Josiah. *An Autobiography of the Rev. Josiah Henson from 1789 to 1881*. Edited by John Lobb. London, ON: Schuyler, Smith & Co. 1881. Henson participated in the defense of western Upper Canada.

Heustis, Daniel D. *A Narrative of the Adventures and Sufferings of Captain Daniel D. Heustis*. Boston: Silas W. Wilder & Co., 1848. Heustis participated in the Hickory Island occupation and the Battle of the Windmill.

Hunt, Jedediah, Jr. *An Adventure on a Frozen Lake*. Cincinnati, OH: Ben Franklin Book and Job Office, 1853. Hunt participated in the Battle of Windsor and escaped.

Landon, Fred. *An Exile from Canada to Van Diemen's Land*. Toronto, ON: Longmans, Green and Company, 1960. Contains letters by Elijah Woodman given to Landon by Woodman's descendants.

Marsh, Robert. *Seven Years of My Life; Or, a Narrative of a Patriot Exile*. Buffalo, NY: Faxon and Stevens, 1847. Marsh joined three Patriot War campaigns: Navy Island, the Battle of Fighting Island and the Battle of Windsor.

McLeod, Donald. *Settlement of Upper Canada*. Cleveland, OH: F.B. Penniman, 1841. McLeod was the senior Patriot War commander in the East.

Miller, Linus W. *Notes of an Exile to Van Diemen's Land*. Fredonia, NY: W. McKinstry & Co., 1846. Miller participated in the Short Hills raid.

Norton, Lewis Adelbert. *Life and Adventures of Colonel L.A. Norton*. Oakland, CA: Pacific Press Publishing House, 1887. Norton played a small role in the Duncombe uprising.

Snow, Samuel. *The Exile's Return*. Cleveland, OH: Smead & Cowles, 1846. Snow fought at the Battle of Windsor.

Sutherland, Thomas Jefferson. *The Trial of Th. J. Sutherland*. Buffalo, NY: Oliver. J. Steele, 1838. Sutherland led the attack on Fort Malden.

Temple, Henry John (Viscount Palmerston). *Correspondence Between Viscount Palmerston & Mr. Stevenson, Relative to the Seizure and Destruction of the Steamboat "Caroline" in the Niagara River, on the Night of the 29th December, 1837, By a Detachment of Her Majesty's Forces from Upper Canada*. Washington, D.C.: U.S. Department of State, 1841. Includes depositions from Gilman Appleby, Captain Andrew Drew and Samuel Wood.

Theller, Dr. Edward. *Canada 1837–38*. Vols. 1 and 2, Philadelphia: Henry F. Anners, 1841. Theller participated in the attack on Fort Malden.

Wait, Benjamin. *Letters from Van Diemen's Land Written During Four Years Imprisonment for Political Offences Committed in Upper Canada*. Buffalo, NY: W.W. Wilgus, 1843. Wait joined the Patriot forces at Navy Island, the Battle of Pelee Island and the Short Hills raid.

Wright, Stephen S. *Narrative and Recollections of Van Diemen's Land During Three Years' Captivity*. Edited by Caleb Lyon. New York: New World Press, 1844. Wright participated in the Battle of the Windmill.

Observers' Accounts

Bonney, Catharina Van Rensselaer. *A Legacy of Historical Gleanings*. Vols. 1 and 2. Albany, NY: J. Munsell, 1875. These contain valuable information on the Van Rensselaer clan and the people they dealt with.

Earl of Durham. *Report on the Affairs of British North America*. London: British House of Commons, February 11, 1839.

Lane, Samuel A. *Fifty Years and Over of Akron and Summit County*. Akron, OH: Summit County Beacon, 1892.

Lindsey, Charles. *Life and Times of Wm. Lyon Mackenzie*. Toronto, ON: P.R. Randall, 1862. Lindsey, Mackenzie's son-in-law, wrote the biography using William's notes.

Martin, Robert Montgomery, ed. "Invasions of Canada from the United States—Battle of Point au Pélé." *Colonial Magazine and Commercial Maritime Journal* 4 (January–April 1841): 350–59.

Palmer, General Friend. *Early Days in Detroit*. Detroit, MI: Hunt & June, 1906.

Historical Accounts

Barnett, Le Roy. *Michigan's Early Military Forces*. Detroit, MI: Wayne State University Press, 2003.

Campbell, C.T. "Settlement of London." In *Transactions, 1909–1911*. London, ON: London and Middlesex Historical Society, 1911.

Carter, John C. "The St. Clair Raids Brought Rebel Conflict Close to Home." *The (Mooretown, ON) Beacon*, December 2012.

Cross, D.W. "The Canadian Rebellion of 1837." *Magazine of Western History Illustrated* 7 (November 1887–April 1888).

Dent, John Charles. *Upper Canadian Rebellion*. Toronto, ON: C. Blackett Robinson, 1885.

Dictionary of Canadian Biography Online (http://www.biographi.ca/index-e.html)

Douglas, R. Alan. *Uppermost Canada: The Western District and the Detroit Frontier, 1800–1850*. Detroit, MI: Wayne State University Press, 2001.

Dunley, Ruth. "In Search of A.D. Smith: A Detective's Quest." *Wisconsin Magazine of History* 89, no. 2 (Winter 2005–2006): 16–27. Dunley makes the link between A.D. Smith, the Hunter's provisional president of Canada, and the later respected jurist of Wisconsin, Abram Daniel Smith.

Greenwood, F. Murray, and Barry Wright, eds. *Rebellion and Invasion of the Canadas, 1837–1839*. Toronto, ON: Toronto University Press, 2002.

Guillet, Edwin G. *The Lives and Times of the Patriots*. Toronto, ON: Ontario Publishing Co., 1963.

Hamilton, Milton W. *The Country Printer: New York State, 1785–1830*. New York: Columbia University Press, 1936. Provides information on early newspaper publishers.

Haydon, James Ryan. *Chicago's True Founder, Thomas J. V. Owen*. Privately published, 1834. Contains information about Henry S. Handy's early years.

Hundey, Ian. "Privileged Scot, Canadian Invader, and Australian Convict: The Story of James Milne Aitchison." *Australasian Canadian Studies* 29, no. 1–2: 49–74.

Johnson, Crisfield. "The Patriot War." In *Centennial History of Erie County, New York*. Buffalo, NY: Matthews & Warren, 1876.

Kinchen, Oscar A. *The Rise and Fall of the Patriot Hunters*. New York: Bookman Associates, 1956. Kinchen's in-depth history of the Hunters unveiled many rare bits of information.

Leach, Hamish A. *A Politico-Military Study of the Detroit River Boundary Defense During the December 1837–March 1838 Emergency*. Doctoral thesis. Windsor, ON: 1963.

Maritime History of the Great Lakes (http://www.maritimehistoryofthegreatlakes.ca)

Moses, John. *A Sketch Account of Aboriginal Peoples in the Canadian Military*. With Donald E. Graves and Warren Sinclair. Ottawa, ON: Department of National Defence Canada, 2004.

Neal, Frederick. *Township of Sandwich (Past and Present)*. Windsor, ON: Record Publishing Co., 1909.

Patterson, Terry. "Hiram Sharp: An American Patriot in the Australian Colonies." *Australasian Canadian Studies* 29, no. 1–2: 29–36.

Rammage, Stuart. *Oakland Township: Two Hundred Years*. vol. 1, and vol. 4, part 2, 1993.

Read, Colin F. *The Rebellion of 1837 in Upper Canada*. Ottawa, ON: Canadian Historical Association, 1988.

———. *The Rising in Western Upper Canada, 1837–38: The Duncombe Revolt and After*. Toronto, ON: University of Toronto Press, 1982.

Read, D.B. *The Canadian Rebellion of 1837*. Toronto, ON: C. Blackett Robinson, 1896.

Ross, Robert B. *The Patriot War*. Detroit, MI: Detroit Evening News, 1890.

Schaffer, Irene. *Henry Woods: The Old Man of the Mountain*. http://www.tasfamily.net.au/~schafferi/index.php?file=kop59.php. This article hints at the fate of Horace Cooley.

Taylor, Professor Dean G. "Captain Findlay Malcolm, Penobscot Loyalist 1783, St. Andrews N.B." *Cataraqui Town Crier* 28, no. 5 (November 2009).

Tiffany, Orrin Edward. *The Relations of the United States to the Canadian Rebellion of 1837–1838*. Edited by Frank Severance. Buffalo, NY: Buffalo Historical Society, 1905.

Wing, Tacott E. "The Patriot War." In *History of Monroe County, Michigan*. New York: Munsell & Company, 1890.

Index

A

Abbey, Dorrephus, hanged 168
aboriginal warriors. *See* native warriors
Aeschylus 132
Aitchison, James
  aids woodman 148
  final story 150
  VDL list 170
Akron 89
  resolutions 35
Allen, David
  VDL list 170
Alway, Robert 19
  life after 157
  released 78
Amherstberg 45
Anderson, Charles 115
  shoots prisoners 116
Anderson, David 24
  death 52
Anderson, Duncan, hanged 168
Anderson, John 92

Anne crew
  captured 49
  defends Sutherland 96
  in Citadel 77
  remaining prisoners released 126
  two escape Fort Henry 92
Appleby, Gilman 87
  at Cleveland convention 85
  bio 89
  life after 157
  tall tales 132
  warned 35
  wounded 35
Arthur, Sir George
  arrives 75
  life after 158
  sends prisoners home 125
  shocked by executions 117
Association of Canadian Refugees 131
Attwood, Israel 121
Australia 150

B

Baby, William
  account of executions 114
  captures ship 49
  Fighting Island 61, 62
  life after 158
  prisoners taken 52
  Windsor battle 101
Bagley, Bernard 85
Baker, Thomas
  VDL list 170
Barber, Sidney
  testifies against 120
Barnum, Henry
  VDL list 170
barracks burned 101
Basden
  in War of 1812 60
Basden, James 60
battles
  Fighting Island 58
  Fort Malden 43
  Montgomery's Tavern 14
  Pelee Island 65

planned 57, 82
Short Hills 71
St. Clair River raids 82
Toronto 13
Windmill 97
Windsor 100
Bedford, Daniel 23
flees 24
hanged list 168
hanging 121
in Windsor raid 99
Bedford, Paul 23
Beemer, Jacob
final story 151
joins rebels 22
VDL list 170
Beemer, Joseph 22
Bellows, Laura 37
Bennett, Uri 115
Berry, John 150
VDL list 170
Bidwell, Marshall 38
Bierce, Lucius 90
at Cleveland convention
85
bio 88
elected commander 86
life after 158
pressured to invade 98
reads proclamation 104
resigns command 129
takes Hume's sword 108
Birge, John 91
Windmill battle 97
Blodget, Orlin
VDL list 170
Boblo Island 45
Bois Blanc Island 45
occupied 47
Bond Head, Sir Francis
14
Boulton, Henry 119
Bowerman, Charles 82
Bradley, Edwin
bio 67

life after 158
Pelee Island 65
Bradley, John
VDL list 170
Brady, Hugh 83
bio 39
confiscates guns 98
message to Basden 60
War of 1812 39
Brady, Philip 127
Brantford 16
Broderick, Edward 116
Brophy, Stephen 92
Brougham, Henry 117
Browne, George, Pelee
Island 68
Brown, George
VDL list 170
Buckley, Christopher,
hanged 168
Buffalo 83
Eagle Tavern 30
welcomes rebels 28
Bugby, Chauncey
final story 151
VDL list 170
Burchall, Sarah 151
Burwell, Mahlon 20
Butler, Orange 38

C

cabin boys 132
Calhoun, Hugh
VDL list 170
Canadian Refugee
Relief Association
(CRRA) 79
Caroline burned 35
Carroll, William 127
Carusi's Saloon 96
Chandler, Samuel
convict labor 138
escapes VDL 145
VDL list 170
Chase, Walter 92

Cheeseman, Benjamin
114
Clark, Albert
hanged list 168
hanging 122
Cleveland 83
convention 85
Miller Block 85
Coffinberry, Salathiel 98
Windsor battle 105
Collins, Robert
VDL list 170
Colonial Advocate 13
consumption 141
Cooley, George
arrived in VDL 138
final story 151
VDL list 170
Cooley, Horace
arrested 83
attempts escape 145
final story 151
VDL list 170
couriers 81
Cronkhite, John
VDL list 170
Culver, Theron
escape fails 95
escapes Citadel 94
released 125
sent to Citadel 77
Cunningham, Cornelius
captured 114
hanged list 168
hanging 122
in Windsor raid 99
leads men at Windsor
105
Curtis, Lysander
VDL list 170

D

Darby, Luther
VDL list 170
Davis, Robert 52

Dawn Township 160
  raided 82
Deal, David 152
Delano, Leonard
  VDL list 170
Dent, John Charles 155
Detroit 83
Doan, Joel 24
Doan, Joshua
  at Fort Malden 24
  bio 24
  captured 114
  hanged list 168
  hanging 123
  in Windsor raid 99
  last letter 123
  reward 24
Dodge, William
  sent to Citadel 77
  wounded 53
Dougall, James
  account of executions
    116
  bio 100
  defends Windsor 106
  Harvell's death 112
  life after 158
Draper, William 77
Dresser, Aaron
  sent home 147
  VDL list 170
Drew, Andrew 34, 41
Drolet, Charles
  helps Theller 92
  life after 159
Dufort 38
Duncombe, Charles
  at Cleveland convention
    85
  bio 15
  flees in disguise 19
  forms CRRA 79
  helps McLeod 60
  leads rebels 16
  life after 159

plans foiled 81
  reward 19
Duncombe uprising
  begins 16
  ends 19
Durfee, Amos 35
Dutcher, Moses
  final story 151
  VDL list 171

E

Eagle Tavern
  Buffalo 30
  Detroit 59
Elliott, William 115
Everett, Edward 147
  paid fare 166
executions 168

F

Family Compact 10
  arrests reformers 19
Fellows, Elon
  VDL list 171
Fero, James
  VDL list 171
Fighting Island
  battle 61
  poorly armed 60
Fitzgibbon, James 74
Fort Erie 90
Fort George 90
Fort Henry
  escape 92
  prisoners transported
    134
Fort Malden 45, 90
Fraer, Michael
  VDL list 171
Franklin, Sir John
  leaves VDL 145
  lectures new prisoners
    139
  life after 159, 160

freelance raids
  Lake Erie 64
  Short Hills 81
  St. Clair River 82
Frères-Chasseurs 79, 84

G

Gates, William
  life after 159
  recalls conversation 155
  recounts VDL arrival
    138
  VDL list 171
Gemmell, James
  describes VDL labor
    141
  escapes VDL 146
  life after 159
  VDL list 171
George, Daniel, hanged
  168
Gilman, John
  VDL list 171
Glasgow, George 60
  artillery 61
  Pelee Island 67
Goodrich, Gideon
  VDL list 171
Goodrich, Harrison 114
  freed 121
Grant, Henry 108
  Harvell's death 111
Grant, John
  customs collector 85
  VDL list 171
Grason, Joseph 121
Greeley, Horace 96
Griggs, Jeremiah
  VDL list 171
Griggs, Nelson
  VDL list 171
Guillet, Edwin 33
Gutridge, John
  VDL list 171

H

Hagerman, Christopher 75
Hamilton 19
Handy, Henry 79
  approaches ACR 131
  bio 37
  cancels invasion 53
  enlists Sutherland 46
  meets reformers 38
  not elected 86
  plans foiled 83
  regains command 129
  Sons of Liberty 80
hangings in London 121
Hansard 114
hard labor 141
Harmon, John
  fires barracks 102
  in Windsor raid 99
  life after 160
  reports on battle 108
Harris, Loving 85
Harvell, Colonel 99
  falls 108
  stories of his death 111
Hay, David 121
Henson, Josiah
  bio 53
  life after 160
Herrington, William 83
Heustis, Daniel
  Buffalo account 135
  describes Franklin 140
  life after 160
  pardon revoked 126
  VDL list 171
Hicks, Garret
  VDL list 171
Higgins, Cornelius 121
Hoadley, Lester
  bio 67
  death 70
  Pelee battle 69

trains troops 65
Hobart Town 138
hogs 132
Holmes, Samuel 70
Horton, Ezra 121
Horton, Joseph 121
House, David
  VDL list 171
House of Lords 114, 117
Hughes, Elizabeth 151
Hull, Henry
  escape fails 95
  escapes Citadel 94
  released 125
  sent to Citadel 77
Hume, John 108
  body multilated 132
Hunter, James 84
Hunters
  lodge convention 85
  lodge eclipses others 84
  lodge focused on
      politics 131
  lodge forms 83
  lodge loses support 130
  lodge members 84
  lodge plans another
      raid 130
  lodge plans invasions
      85
  transported 134
Hunt, Jedediah
  bio 100
  describes battle 106
  escapes to Detroit 114
  flees Windsor 113
  Harvell's death 112
  life after 160
  Windsor battle 104

I

Ingles, James
  VDL list 171
Irvine, John 137

J

Jackson, Andrew 9, 37
Jackson, Philip 127
Johnson, Lieutenant
      William 132
Johnson, Richard 85
Johnston, Bill 85
  commodore 86
Jones, William 121
July 4
  invasion plans 81
  invasion plans foiled 81

K

Kennedy, David 121
Kerry, William 82

L

Lambton, John George.
      See Lord Durham
Lane, Samuel
  Harvell's death 112
  joins Patriots 35
Lapan, Charlie 110
Lawless Aggressions Act
      73, 119
  changed 128
Lawton, Sylvester,
      hanged 168
Leach, Lyman, hanged
      168
Leeper, Andrew
  VDL list 171
Leforte, Joseph
  VDL list 171
Les Patriotes 79
  at convention 85
Lett, Benjamin
  bio 63
  life after 161
  Pelee Island 65
Lewiston 131
lies and propaganda 132

Lindsey, Charles 33
Liscum, Daniel
  VDL list 172
Lockport 79, 130
lodges, secret 80
London 19, 78
  meeting 20
Loop, Hiram
  VDL list 172
Lord Durham 130, 154
  report 154
Lord Glenelg 16, 126
  Sutherland case 75
Lount, Samuel 77
  hanged list 168
Lynn, Hiram
  hanged list 169
  hanging 121
  trial 119

M

Mabee, Orin 121
Macaulay, James 127
Mace, Isaac 127
Mackenzie, Alexander 79
Mackenzie, Diogenes 127
Mackenzie, William Lyon
  attacks Toronto 13
  bio 12
  CRRA 79
  forms another group
    131
  in prison 131
  in Washington 96
  life after 161
  visited by Wright 166
MacNab, Allan 14
  arrests rebels 19
  life after 161
  Navy Island 33
  supresses rebels 17
Maitland, John 60, 74, 83
  death 70
  Pelee Island 68

Malcolm family 21
  Augustus 22
  Daniel 22
  Eddy 22
  Eliakim 21
  Eliakim, life after 161
  Eliakim, pardoned 23
  Finlay I 21
  Finlay II 21, 22
  Finlay III 21
  Finlay III, acquitted 22
  Isaac 21
  James Jr. 22
  James, pardoned 23
  John 22
  Norman 22
  Peter 22
  Peter, convicted 22
  Shubael 22
  those not involved 22
Mallory, Norman
  arrived in VDL 138
  VDL list 172
Marentette, Pierre 108
  life after 162
  saves captain 110
  shoots Harvell 112
Marsh, Robert
  bio 37
  captured 114
  describes battle 107,
    109
  describes Franklin 139
  Fighting Island 62
  flees Windsor 113
  Harvell's death 111
  has misgivings 105
  life after 162
  Navy Island 37
  trial 120
  VDL list 172
  Windsor battle 102
Martin, Foster
  VDL list 172
Martin, Jeheil

  VDL list 172
Masons 25
  aid VDL escape 146
  aid Woodman 148
  also Hunters 84
  anti 29
  Duncombe 15
  Roberts 39
  William Putnam 20
Mason, Stevens 42
  Hunter member 85
Mathers, Calvin
  VDL list 172
Mathers, Chauncey
  VDL list 172
Matthews, Peter 77
  hanged list 169
McCarrick, William 127
McCartan, Thomas 70
McDougall, David
  testifies against 121
McFarlan, Robert
  Fighting Island 61
  winter march 58
McIntyre, John 127
McLeod, Alexander
  VDL list 172
McLeod, Donald 79
  account of executions
    114
  at Cleveland convention
    85
  bio 57
  flees in disguise 63
  forms CRRA 79
  Harvell's death 111
  Hunters Lodge 83
  in War of 1812 57
  letter to Van Rensselaer
    72
  life after 162
  march 58
  plans foiled 81
  secretary of war 87
  works with Handy 129

McMartin, Sheriff
    Alexander 126
McNulty, John
    VDL list 172
Meadow, Stephen 121
Milard, Fanny 24
  visits husband before
      hanging 123
militia
  at Toronto 14
  black company 53
  board the *Anne* 47
  board the *Caroline* 34
  limited numbers 45
  mistaken for regulars
    106
  supported by regulars
    60
Miller Block 85
Miller, Edwin 70
Miller, Linus
  attempts escape 145
  Canton account 136
  describes Franklin 140
  recalls flogging 143
  VDL list 172
Miller, Stephen 116
Milles, William 102
Montgomery, John 13,
    92, 131
Montreal 83
Moore, Andrew
  VDL list 172
Moore, Elias 19
  bailed 78
  life after 163
Morden, Gilbert 92
Morin, Michael
  VDL list 172
Morreau, James, hanged
    169
Morrisette, John
  VDL list 172
Mott, Benjamin 138
Myers, Isaac 127

N

native warriors 17, 33,
    45, 82, 129
  end prisoner executions
    116
  Windsor 110
Navy Bay 134
Navy Island
  abandoned 41
  battle 32
  occupied 30
Neal, Frederick 112
Nelson, Robert 79, 87
  Lower Canada invasion
    97
neutrality law 40
Noah, Mordecai 39
Norton, Lewis
  bio 26
  in uprising 27
Norwich 17, 23, 27
Nottage, William
  VDL list 172
Nugent's Inn 82

O

Oakland 21
Owen, Alson
  VDL list 172

P

Paddock, Jacob
  VDL list 172
Panic of 1837 10, 25
pardons granted 147
Parish, Thomas 70
Parker, Chauncey
  escape fails 94
  released 125
  sent to Citadel 77
Partridge, Abraham
  released 126
  sent to Citadel 77

Patriot Masons 84
Patriots
  diverse membership 36
  ship captured 47
  steal weapons 42
Peach Island 43
Peeler, Joel, hanged 169
Pelee Island
  battle 67
  casualties 71
  prisoners tried and
    released 127
Perley, Amos
  hanged list 169
  hanging 123
Pew, Benjamin
  released 125
  sent to Citadel 77
Phelps, Russell, hanged
    169
Pierce James
  VDL list 172
Polly, Ira
  final story 152
  VDL list 172
Port Arthur 145
Priest, Asa
  VDL list 173
Prince, John
  abuses Theller 55
  arrests Sutherland 74
  bio 55
  executes prisoners 114
  exonerated 117
  life after 163
prisoners
  fates unknown 150
  list who hanged 168
  radicalized 19
  released 83
  some leave VDL 148
  transported 134
Proudfoot, William 124
Putnam, George
  testifies against 121

Putnam, William 86
  arrested 20
  bio 20
  death 109
  flees 20
  leads men at Windsor 105
  Mason 20
Pybus, Cassandra 151

Q

Quakers 24, 123, 163

R

rebellion
  begins 12
  causes 9
  conclusion 155
red flags on ice 61
Reed, Charles 121
Republican Bank of
      Canada 87
Reynolds, Solomon
  VDL list 173
Reynolds, William
  final story 152
  VDL list 173
Richardson, Asa
  VDL list 173
Rideau Canal 134
Rideout, George 127
Rising Sun Tavern 59
Roberts, Elijah 81, 98
  angry at Theller 47
  bio 39
  joins Patriots 39
  life after 163
Robinson, John 76, 127
Rochester 83, 131
Root, Erastus 39
Ross, Robert 63, 69, 71
Russell, George 63

S

Sandusky 58
Sandy Bay 138
Scotland 21
Scott, Winfield 41
secret societies 79
Seward, H.C.
  Pelee Island 65
  replaced by Bradley 66
Sharp, Hiram
  final story 152
  VDL list 173
Sheldon, Chauncey
  trial 120
  VDL list 173
Sherwood, Henry 76, 119
  life after 163
Shew, Henry 148
  VDL list 173
ships
  Anne 42
  Anne captured 48
  Barcelona 41
  Buffalo 83, 134
  Canton 134
  Caroline 34
  Champlain 99
  Constitution 90, 157
  Erie 59
  Marquis of Hastings 134
  Steiglitz 147
  Sultana 157
  Thames 105
  Young Eagle 148
Short Hills 22, 83
Simmons, John
  VDL list 173
Smith, Abram
  at Cleveland convention 85
  bio 89
  elected president 85
  life after 163
Smith, Lydia 39

Smith, Nathaniel
  released 126
  sent to Citadel 77
Smith, Orin
  VDL list 173
Snow, Samuel
  bio 99
  captured 114
  describes battle 107
  describes trials 120
  life after 164
  VDL list 173
  Windsor battle 103
Sombra 82
Sons of Liberty 80
Sparta 24, 123
Spartan Rangers 27
Spencer, Silvanus 74
Sprague, John
  VDL list 173
St. Albans 83
Stevens, Elizur
  VDL list 173
Stewart, Joseph
  attempts escape 145
  final story 152
  VDL list 173
Stewart, Riley
  VDL list 173
Stockton, Thomas
  VDL list 173
Stone, Benjamin 85
Sugar Island 46
  generals arrive 53
Sutherland, Thomas
  arrested 74
  arrives in Michigan 45
  bio 29
  court-martial 75
  goes west 41
  life after 164
  refutes Theller 96
  released 126

  sent to Citadel 76

takes weapons 56
Swanburg, John
  VDL list 173
Sweet, Alvin
  VDL list 173
Sweetman, Daniel
  testifies against 120
Swete, Sylvanus, hanged 169
swine 132
Symonds, Thomas 70

T

Taylor, David 167
Texas Revolution 10
Thames burned 105
Thayer, Squire
  aids Theller escape 94
  life after 164
  released 125
  sent to Citadel 77
Theller, Edward
  attacks town on *Anne* 46
  avoids hanging 77
  bio 38
  captured 49
  commands ship 46
  defends himself 76
  in Washington 96
  joins Patriots 38
  life after 165
  plans Citadel escape 92
  sent to Citadel 77
  slanders Sutherland 96
  tall tales 132
  trial 76
Thomas, John
  VDL list 173
Thompson, David 76
Thompson, Joseph
  VDL list 173
ticket of leave 143
Tiffany, Abraham 121

Townsend, Henry 60
Treason Act 73
tuberculosis 141
Tyrrell, John
  VDL list 174

U

Upper Canada
  defense force 1838 130
  government 9
  improved defenses 60
  numbers arrested 167
  passes new law 73

V

Van Buren, Martin 36, 96
Van Camp, Garret
  VDL list 174
Van Diemen's Land 133
  former governor 75
  last man to leave 150
  named changed 22
  natives 143
  prisoner clothes 141
  prisoner food 141
  prisoner labor 141
  prisoners arrive 137
  sea journey to 135
  three escape 145
  ticket of leave 143
Van Edmond, Anthony 167
Van Rensselaer, Henry
  bio 72
  death 70
  Pelee battle 69
  trains troops 65
Van Rensselaer, Kilian 72
Van Rensselaer, Rensselaer 30
  issues order 45
  life after 165

Navy Island 33
Vernon, John
  arrived in VDL 138
  VDL list 174
von Schoultz, Nils
  bio 90
  hanged list 169
  plans invasion 90
Vreeland, John 58
  fails again 66
  hides weapons 60
  sentenced 82

W

Waggoner, James
  arrived in VDL 138
  VDL list 174
Wait, Benjamin
  bio 71
  convict labor 138
  escapes VDL 145
  life after 165
  Pelee Island 72
  VDL list 174
Wait, Maria 165
Warner, Benjamin 127
War of 1812
  Battle of Malcolm's Mill 21
  Fort Malden 43
  native warriors 129
  Putnam in 20
Washburn, Samuel
  final story 152
  VDL list 174
Western District 45
Western District, limited defense 45
western uprising
  begins 16
  ends 19
White Patrick
  VDL list 174
Whiting, Nathan

VDL list 174
Whitney, Riley
  VDL list 174
Whitney, Robert 121
Wilkins, Ross 47
  life after 166
  sentences Vreeland 82
Williams, James
  VDL list 174
Williams, John
  VDL list 174
Williams, John C. 121
Williams, Nathan 85
Wilson, Ann 38
Wilson, Edward
  VDL list 174
Wilson, James 42
Windsor battle
  barracks burned 101
  begins 100
  captives tried 119
  disposition of prisoners
      121
  invaders flee 113
  orchard clash 106
  prisoners freed 120
  prisoners hanged 121
Woodbury, Bemis
  VDL list 174
Woodbury, Trueman 121
Woodman, Elijah
  bio 24
  captured 114
  dies at sea 149
  flees 26
  leaves VDL 148
  lifts mens' spirits 142
  Mason 25
  trial 120
  VDL list 174
Woodruff, Martin, hanged
      169
Wood, Samuel 35
  deposition 29
  gives testimony 127

Pelee Island 70
  winter march 59
Woods, Henry 151
Worth, William 58
Wright, Stephen
  life after 166
  recalls flogging 142
  sent home 147
  VDL list 174

Y

Young, Selah 147

About the Author

Shaun McLaughlin maintains two history blogs: one on the Patriot War, and one on William Johnston, the Thousand Islands legend. A researcher, journalist and technical writer for over thirty years, with a master's degree in journalism, he lives on a hobby farm in eastern Ontario. Now a semiretired freelance writer, he focuses on fiction and nonfiction writing projects. This is his second book for The History Press.

Visit us at
www.historypress.net
....
This title is also available as an e-book